The Ongoing Adventures of
ASBO Jesus
by JON BIRCH

FOREWORD

ASBO Jesus is ... defiant, disturbing, radical, contemporary, irreverent and offensive ... Just like Jesus so often was and is! I think it was William Temple that said of the church that it should be the place that "comforted the disturbed and disturbed the comfortable". ASBO Jesus has that effect! You won't agree with the sentiment of Jon's ASBO Jesus all the time ... but iron sharpens iron and you will find your assumptions, stereotypes and theology stretched and challenged. Like the story of "The Emperor's New Clothes" ASBO Jesus cuts to the chase to show us the fallacy of our sacred cows and our fondly held prejudices, it reveals the simplicity of a belief system that might just as well be summed up as love.

The ASBO Jesus cartoons are a work of contemporary art in themselves; simple, stark and attention grabbing and I believe that what they convey is of serious importance. In an age when it seems that God is being overlaid with the cultural veneers of consumption, emotionalism, celebrity obsession, entertainment, individualism and prosperity, ASBO Jesus appears like a ragged prophet questioning the moral landscape, undermining complacency and reminding that faith is a red blooded call to service and not an institutional call to services!

I have known Jon for some thirty years and I know that his work and art are borne of a journey rooted in an authentic desire to understand and pursue a 'Kingdom' perspective at the expense of 'Christendom'. Jon doesn't shy away from the themes and issues that we might rather ignore or avoid; he digs in the dirt of personal, social, political, institutional and religious pain and hypocrisy. He underlines the duplicity of complacent religion and is a voice in the wilderness declaring that comfortable Christianity is an oxymoron! Perhaps the truest act of his loyalty to the Kingdom of God is that his unbridled satire and cynicism allows us space to ask ourselves what we really believe... provided we can move beyond the occasional moments of defensiveness that he provokes!

The origins of ASBO Jesus are connected to a campaign that Frontier Youth Trust (FYT) established six years ago. FYT wanted to undermine the negative stereotyping that continues to blight marginalised young people in our society to this day. One of the ways that the campaign developed was that young people were awarded ASBO certificates that affirmed them as Alright, Sensational, Beautiful and Original. With this foreword I am presenting one of these certificates to Jon (who remains eternally young!) for this book! I make this award not because he is donating a percentage of the price of the book to FYT (!) but for his honesty, humour, candour, integrity, insight and for sharing ASBO Jesus with us ... reminding us that Jesus is NOT a tame lion!

Dave Wiles (CEO: Frontier Youth Trust)

ENDORSEMENTS

"Like the boy who pointed out that the emperor was naked, Jon's cartoons seem to cut through hype and hypocrisy and simply tell things the way they are. ASBO Jesus is always thought provoking, often hilarious, sometimes painful and Jon is such a gracious and generous host in the discussions that ensue."
Jenny Baker.

"Consistently, the cartoons of ASBO Jesus are perfectly executed little messages that carry a punch. They are like a Trojan horse that I invite in with curiosity, only to discover that they contain something that may very well undo me."
David Hayward, AKA The Naked Pastor.

"ASBO Jesus is satirical. ASBO Jesus makes you laugh, makes you cry and tugs on your guilt strings. ASBOJesus is a modern day prophet... but has a better sense of humour than Isaiah."
Carole Hawkins.

"I tried for years to get good community conversation going on my blog, ASBO Jesus manages it with one cartoon, I'm so glad to be part of it. Funny, painful, irritating, unbalanced, insightful, ignatian... no, scrap the last one, but Jon's all the rest!"
Caroline Ramsey.

"At a time when I felt alienated & disassociated with the church I stumbled upon ASBO Jesus. I prefer honest, distinctive and genuine people, I found this in Jon and the group of ASBOers who come and go sharing their tears and joy. That's why I choose to stay. The art speaks for itself... Simple, powerful and sensitive."
Dennis Coburn, AKA Dennis the Mennis.

"With a critical eye and loving heart, Jon Birch tears apart the Christian industrial complex that churns out faith fast food. In the process, he reveals those rare glimpses of God hidden among mounds of Jesus junk."
Becky Garrison,
author of 'Jesus Died for This?: A Satirist's Search for the Risen Christ.'

"Funny thing about Jesus and ASBOs; whilst governments can create, issue, and rescind ASBOs, there is nothing they can do to alter Jesus' state of being; he will do what he wants to, where he wants to, when he wants to, with whom he wants to, and eternally be to governments the annoyance of being a force beyond their control."
Forrest Scott Wood.

"Economical in style but expansive in content, Jon's simple vector cartoons pack a powerful punch: Prepare to be amused, enraged and challenged!"
Pat Bennet.

"ASBO Jesus has been a place where, with the help of the other regular contributors, I have been able to explore the reality behind the 'accepted' and rather hackneyed facade of Christian faith... and to gradually disentangle myself from the mess left by the well-meaning, but (I now believe) misguided faith community in which I grew up."
Johnny Branston.

"ASBO cartoons are all about tea-spitting humour, with the relief filled, wobbly-smiled recognition that someone else sometimes sees the world the same way you do. More importantly, they are made by a real human being - more real than most - who is prepared to pour his heart, soul and angst into his work, along with his doubts, fears, passions and joy. Such a courageous approach results in work that is honest, relational, and deeply relevant."
James Milne, AKA Linus.

"With ASBO Jesus, Jon has managed to create a space in which it is OK to question and grow without the fear that so often comes with Christian discourse. Jon has challenged and stretched my faith through his often humorous view of Christianity and the world around him, but also nourished my faith with love and gentle prodding."
Revd Robb Sutherland.

"ASBO Jesus has a unique way of challenging and critiquing the church. Jon's cartoons are both humorous and thought provoking. It's fantastic to see them as a book."
Sonia Mainstone-Cotton.

"Jon's cartoons are spiky but their author isn't. He just loves the church and, like the prophets of old, wants us to notice our faults."
Revd Anne Stewart.

"Every now and then I find myself thinking about something, then, lo and behold, ASBO Jesus has a cartoon on exactly that theme; highly spooky or the Holy Spirit?! Sometimes laugh out loud funny and simultaneously thought-provoking, sometimes tear-jerkingly vulnerable and challengingly honest. Jon's cartoons continually inspire and encourage me in my own ministry."
Revd Catriona Gorton.

"Funny, moving and provoking, but always grounded in love and a sense of companionship, ASBO Jesus quite often takes the questions right out of my mouth!"
Ellie, AKA These Old Shades.

NOTES FROM THE AUTHOR

Phew, it's finally here! It seems to have taken me an age to get it finished. And now it's done I just hope you enjoy it.

I want to take this opportunity to thank everyone who has been to the blog, to take part in conversation, to take time out to encourage others, to make comment, often challenging, often wise, often thoughtful, sometimes bonkers. Thank you to all of you, because without you there really would be no ASBO Jesus.

There are a few important acknowledgements I need to make. Firstly my mum. She would have enjoyed many of these cartoons and possibly rolled her eyes at others. It was after her death that I started doing them as a way to keep my mind occupied. How could I have known that it would grow as it has? ASBO Jesus has been something of a catharsis for me and I have been amazed to discover just how many others have found it helpful too. Amazing. Secondly, Clare, my ever loving, ever loyal wife. It was she who came up with the name ASBO Jesus... I wasn't too keen on the name to begin with... How wrong was I?! Thanks Clare for sharing the ride, the joy, the sadness, the bright and the bleak. You are a treasure. Thirdly, thanks to Jonny Baker for encouraging me to start blogging and for being a constant and unchanging friend... The best kind of friend. Fourthly and lastly and while I'm on the subject of constant friends, thanks to Dave Wiles. An inspiration for many years. It also happens that he is CEO of Frontier Youth Trust, a charity working with young people on the margins of society. I love the work this organisation does and am proud that 10% of the profits of this book will be going to help their work.

It is to all the above that I dedicate this book with love and gratitude. Mum, Clare, Jonny, Dave and all ASBOers everywhere! Thank you, lovely people.

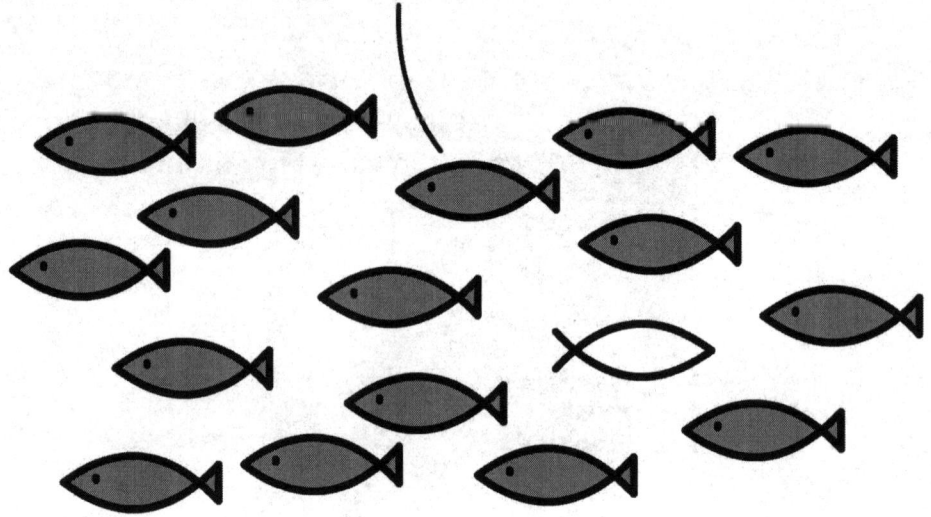

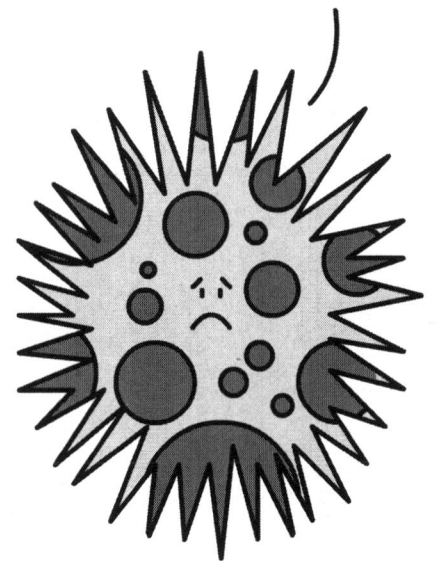

PUZZLE PAGE

Which of these cool items are *essential* when putting on an alternative worship service?

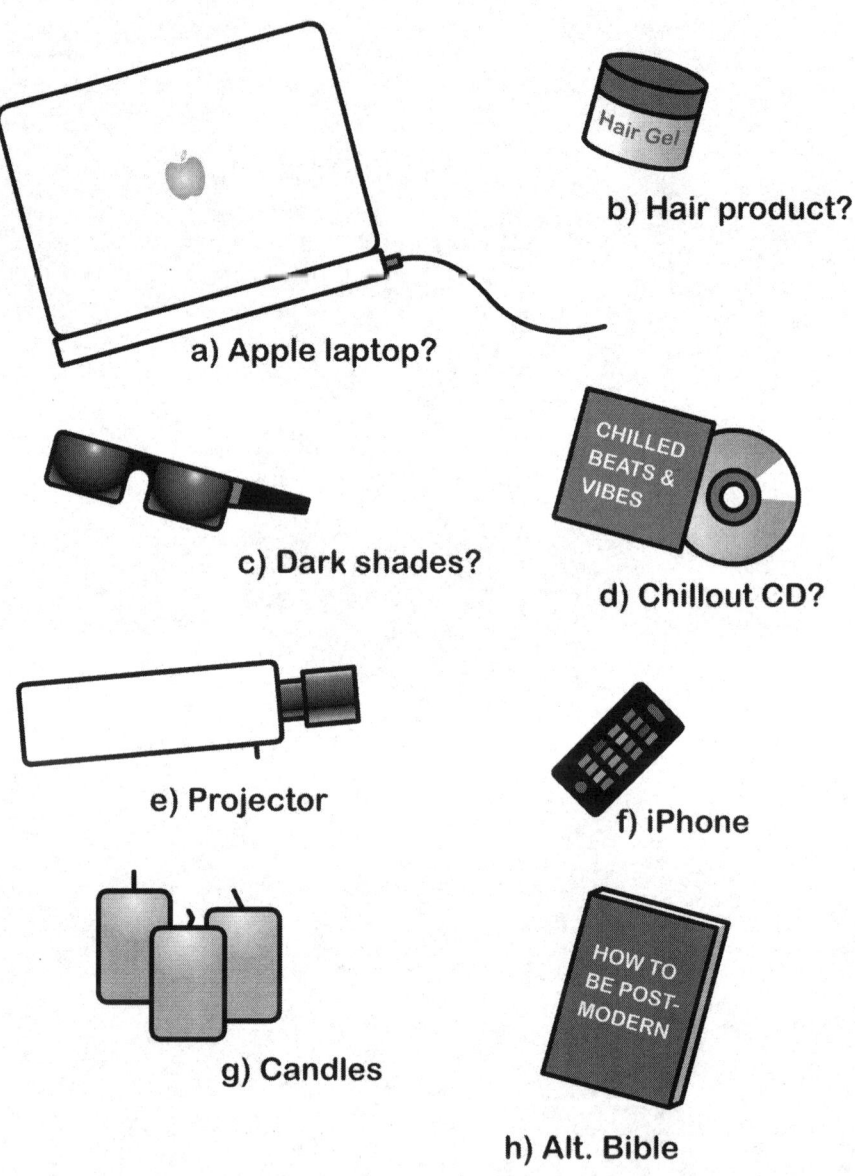

a) Apple laptop?
b) Hair product?
c) Dark shades?
d) Chillout CD?
e) Projector
f) iPhone
g) Candles
h) Alt. Bible

All of these items are essential.

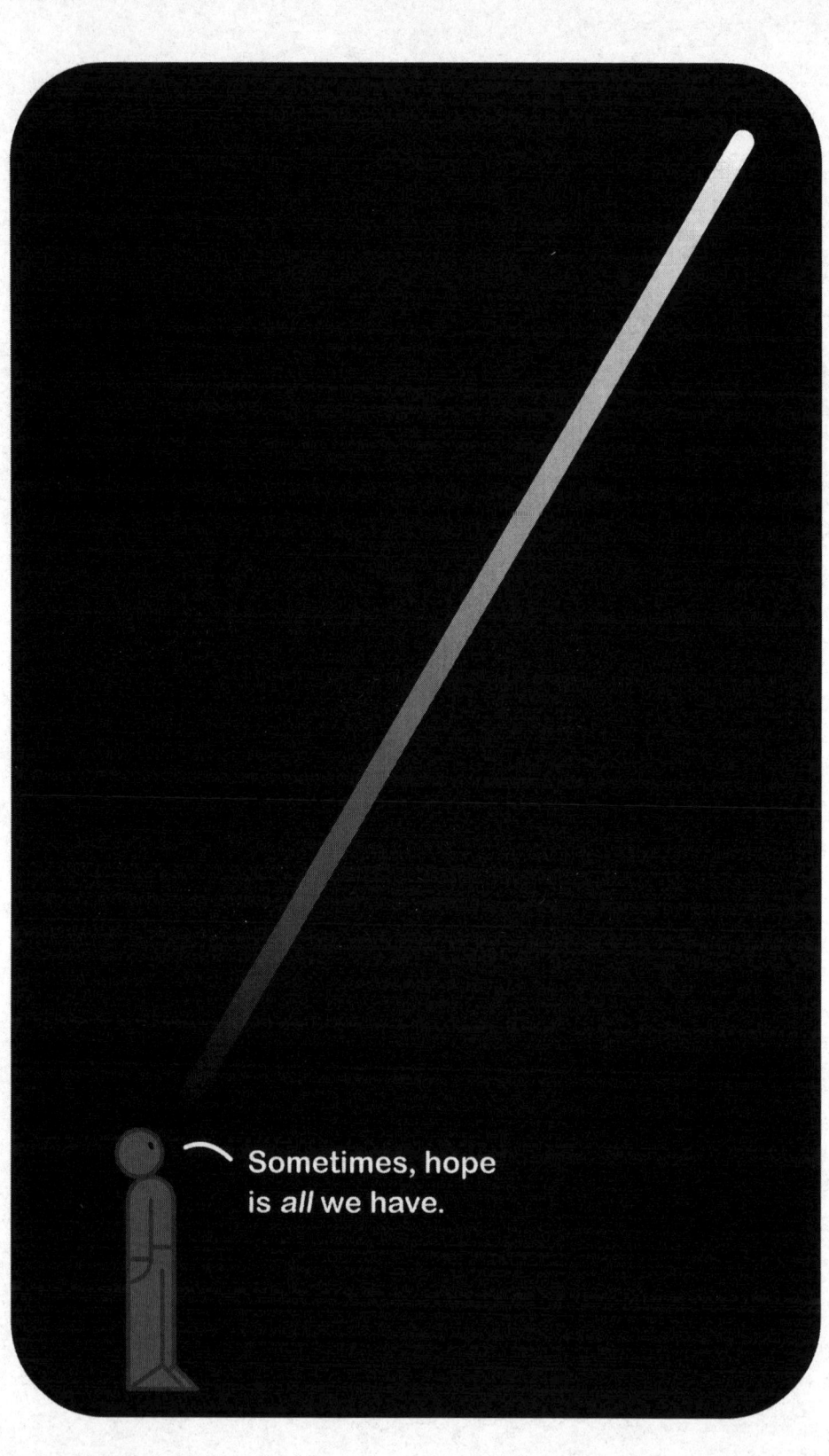

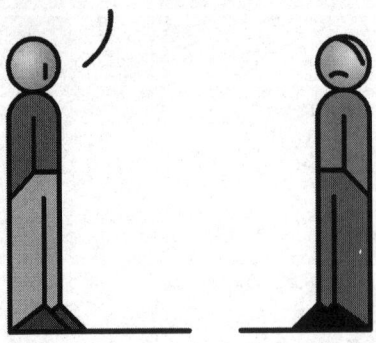
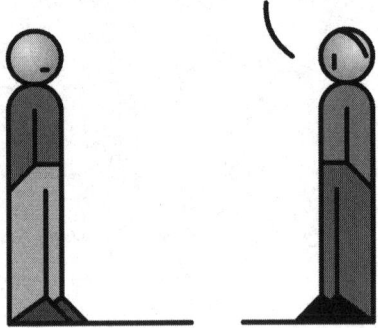
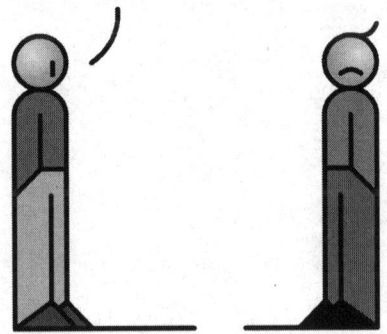

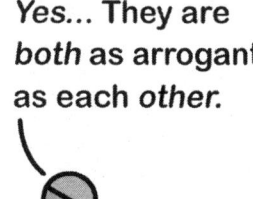

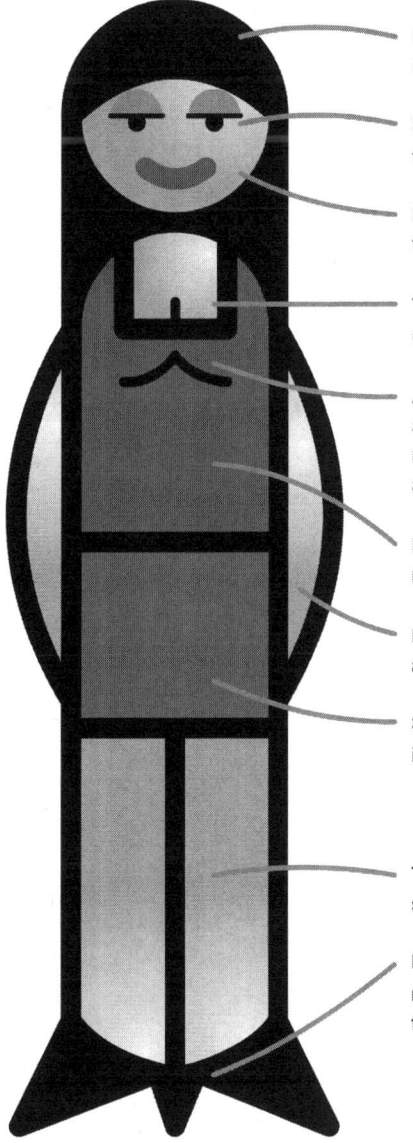

Can you see where this Christian woman is going wrong?

- Raven hair, worn loose, in a suggestive manner.
- Subtle eye shadow gives her that 'come to bed' look.
- Lipstick, a primitive sexual device that Jezebel would be proud of.
- The merest hint of cleavage has led to the down fall of many a poor defenseless male.
- A sensible, less comfortable bra would also alleviate male attention. Remember, men do not have breasts and that is why they stare at them.
- Red is the colour of prostitution. Sombre, more muted tones are much more suitable.
- Naked flesh is never desirable and should be avoided at all costs.
- Skirts worn above the knee are a no-no and invariably lead to acts of a sinful nature.
- Thick, dark nylon tights or a lengthy skirt should be worn at all times.
- Even the tiniest of heals will threaten a small man. A true woman of God will always wear flat shoes.

Being a woman is not her fault... displaying it *is!*

One dull sermon too many.
Even for an empty church.

Just once more around the churchyard and the new minister would be broken in.

THIS WONDERFUL BOOK CONTAINS IMPORTANT TOPICS FOR THE 21ST CENTURY CHRISTIAN, SUCH AS:

- How to appear fine when really you are distressed.
- How to get up on Sunday when everything in you wants to stay in bed.
- How to pretend to be interested in the problems of others.
- The church service and how to survive it.

+ Tips on how to look disapprovingly upon youngsters, how to manipulate those in authority and how to carry on an adulterous affair without anyone finding out.

THIS EDITION ALSO INCLUDES A SECTION ON THE NEEDS OF THE POOR AND HOW BEST TO AVOID THEM.

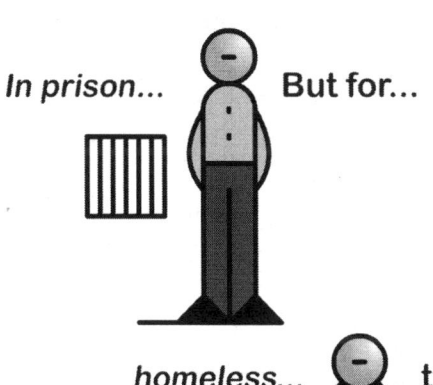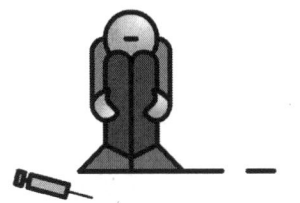

Sunday morning worship.

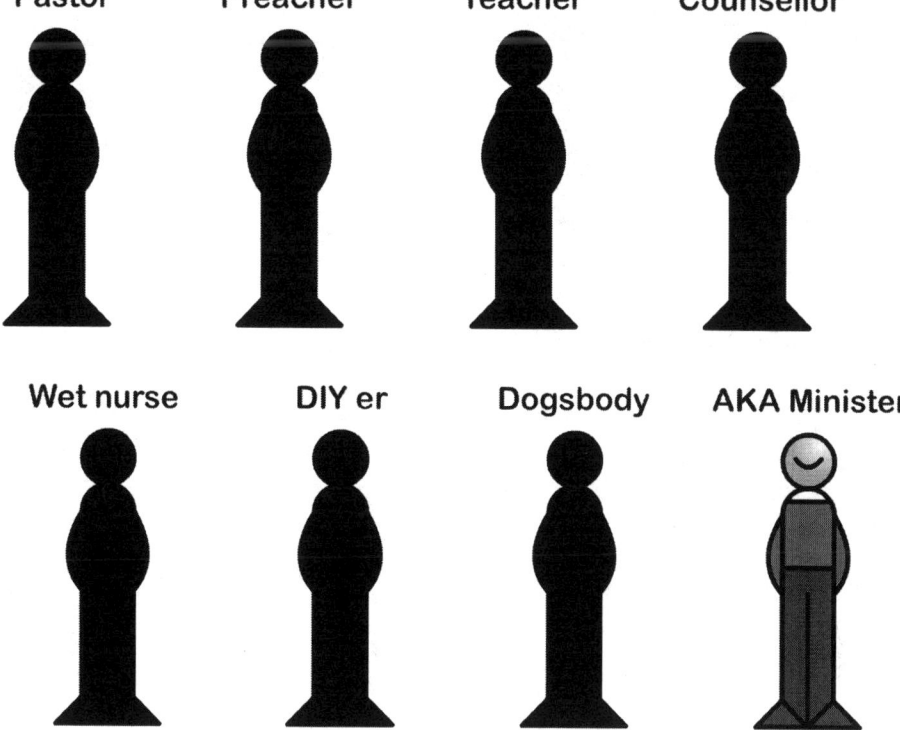

Whilst 'catching the fire'...

...Jimmy was burnt to a crisp.

PUZZLE PAGE

Eric the church mouse is making a new nest, but he needs materials with which to make it. What would you like him to nibble his way through first?

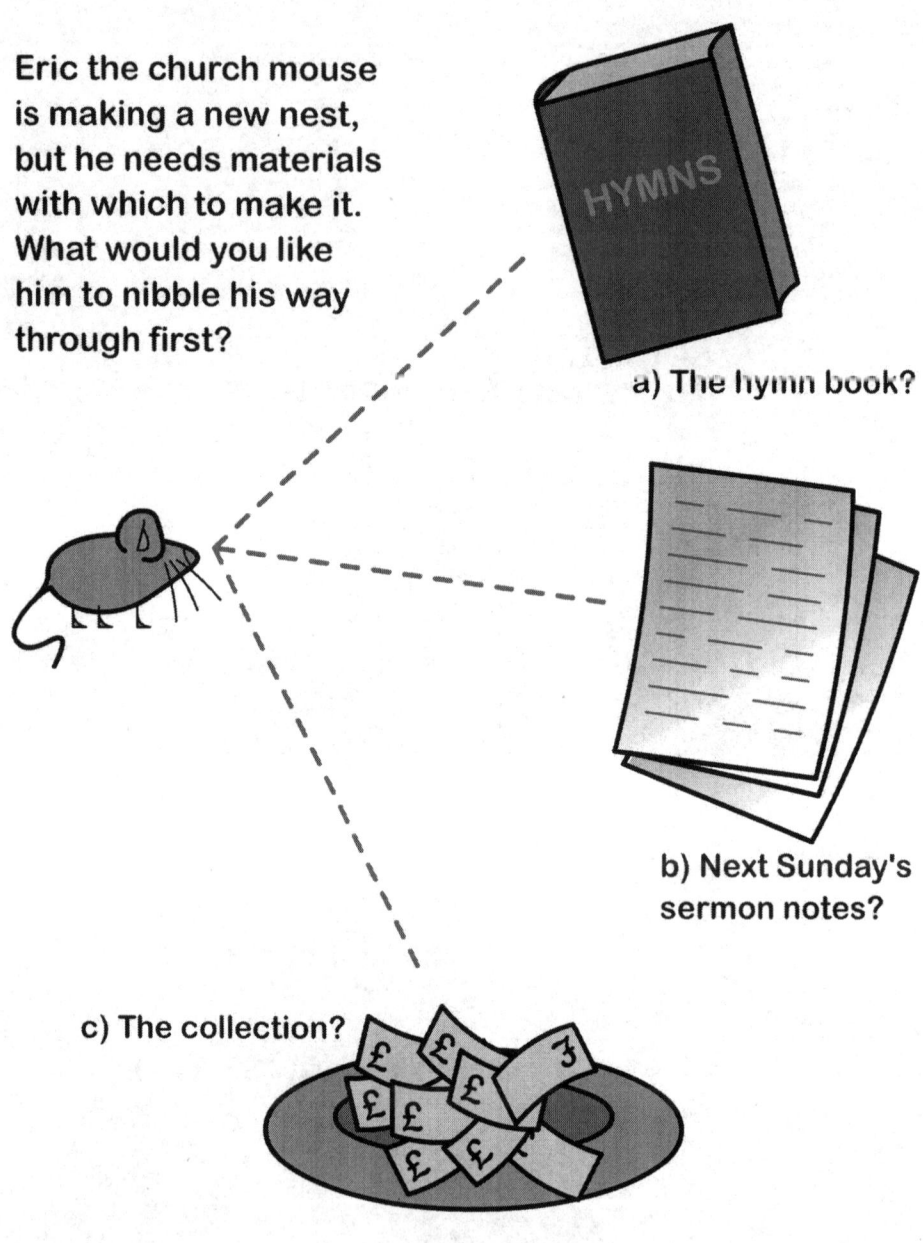

a) The hymn book?

b) Next Sunday's sermon notes?

c) The collection?

If you chose 'c', then you made the choice of a true radical.

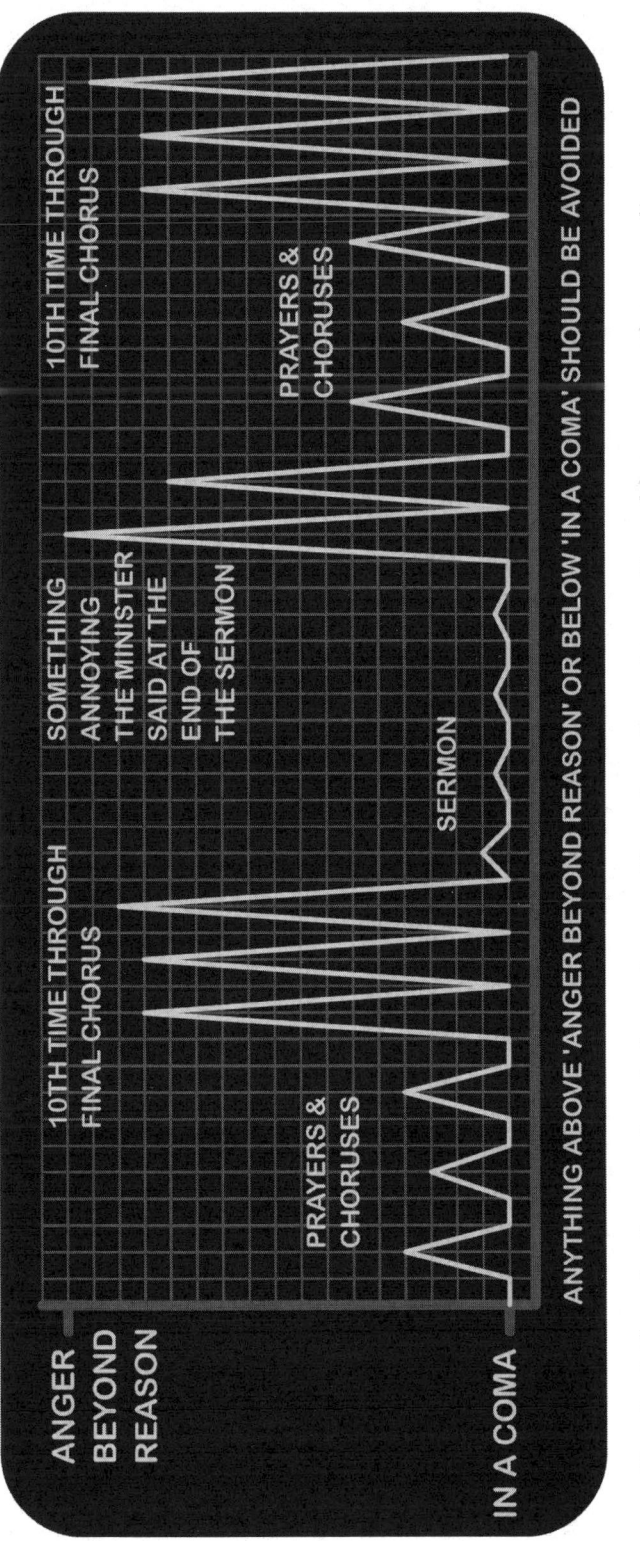

For last Sunday's service I rigged myself up to a heart monitor. Above are the results.

10.30am MORNING SERVICE
Well, we call it a 'service', but I'm not really sure *who* it serves.

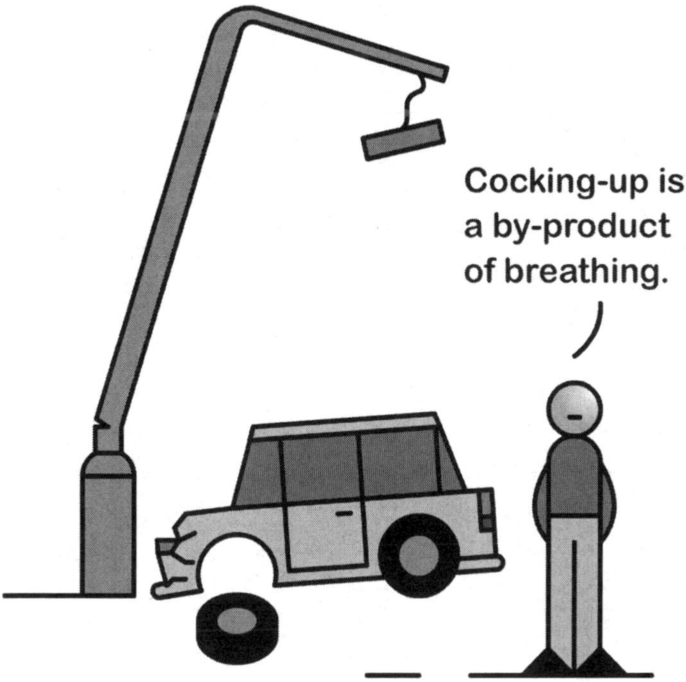
Cocking-up is
a by-product
of breathing.

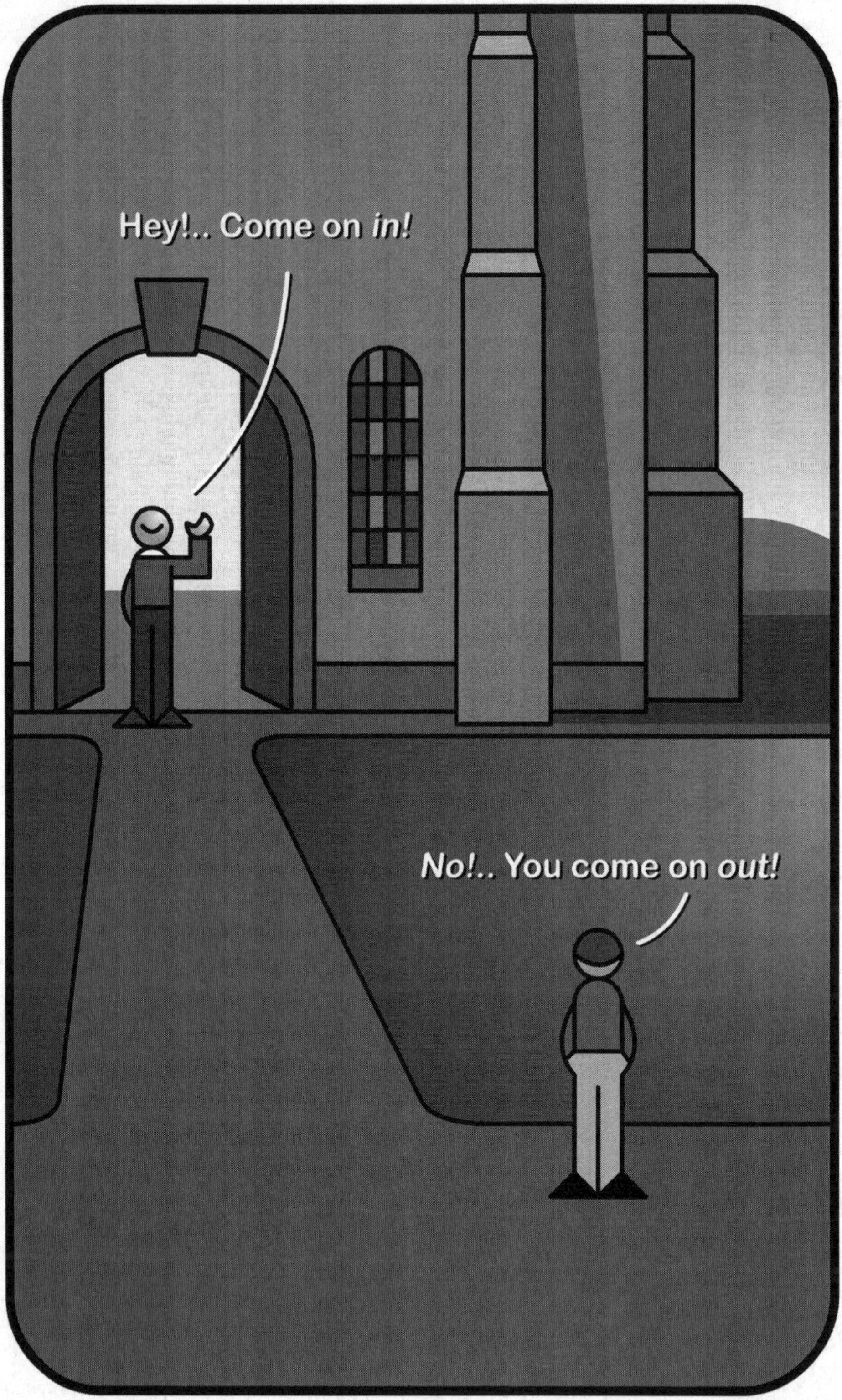
Hey!.. Come on *in!*
No!.. You come on *out!*

I come from a completely *normal* family...

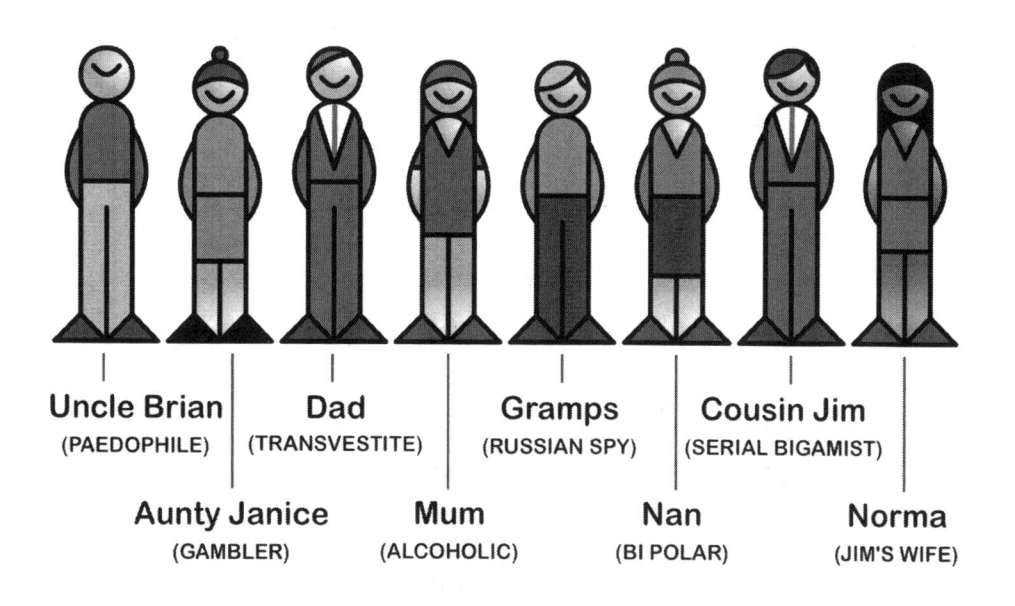

Uncle Brian	Dad	Gramps	Cousin Jim
(PAEDOPHILE)	(TRANSVESTITE)	(RUSSIAN SPY)	(SERIAL BIGAMIST)

Aunty Janice	Mum	Nan	Norma
(GAMBLER)	(ALCOHOLIC)	(BI POLAR)	(JIM'S WIFE)

Jesus commands and creation obeys...

I command and...

SIT!

NO!

It's Prof. Dawkins!..
He says he's *sorry*
and can he *please*
come in?!

NEW CREATION

ANXIETY! WORRY! GUILT! STRESS! FEAR!

The silence is deafening.

We must *not* cross this line of *decent* human behaviour.
What *line*?
!

If I let myself *cry*, I fear I'll *never* stop.

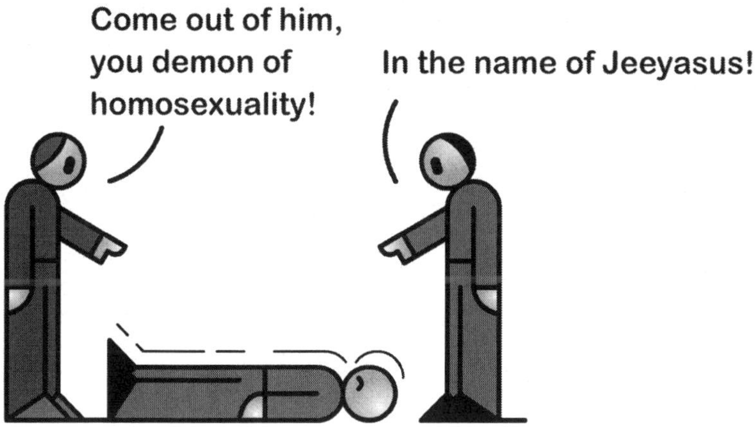

Five minutes later...

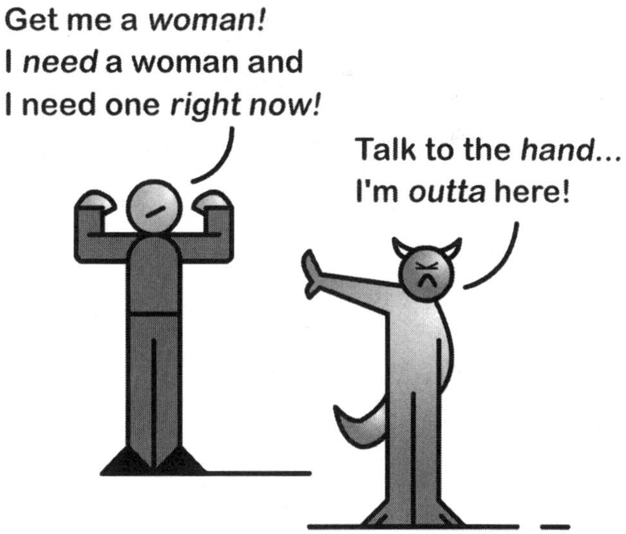

So, Doctor...
What do you think is the cause behind the recent swine flu outbreak?
It is God's judgement that *all* sinners *die* like *pigs!*
!

I'm sorry, but you really *shouldn't* be that surprised that some people in this church immediately judge you. After all, you have had *twelve children* with *four different mothers!*
In our faith, that simply *isn't* done.

Jacob, son of Isaac,
meets the pastor.

Man, I'm disillusioned.

...What happens when you live under an illusion.

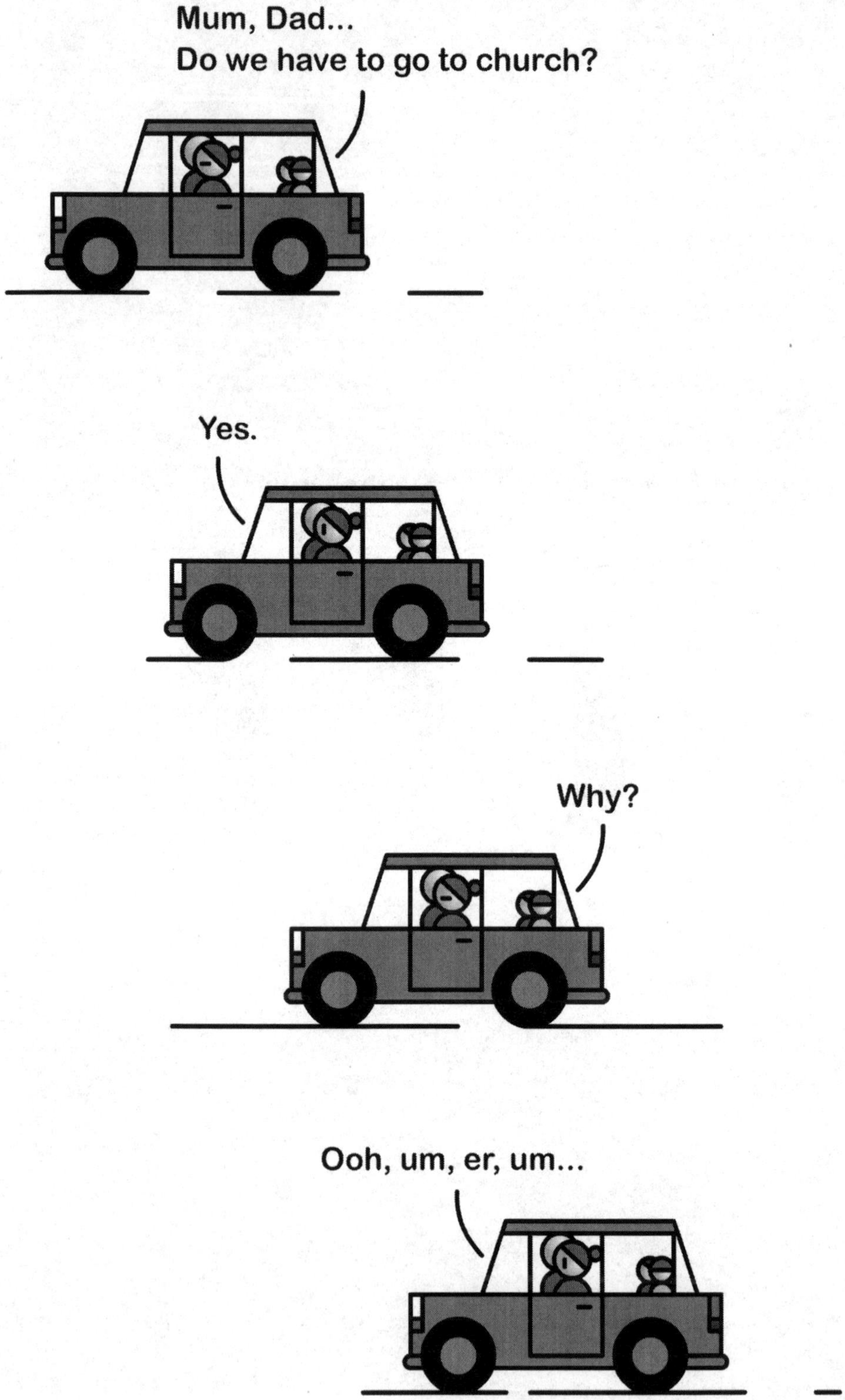
Mum, Dad...
Do we have to go to church?
Yes.
Why?
Ooh, um, er, um...

"All the darkness in the world
cannot put out the light
of a single candle."

Saint Francis of Assisi

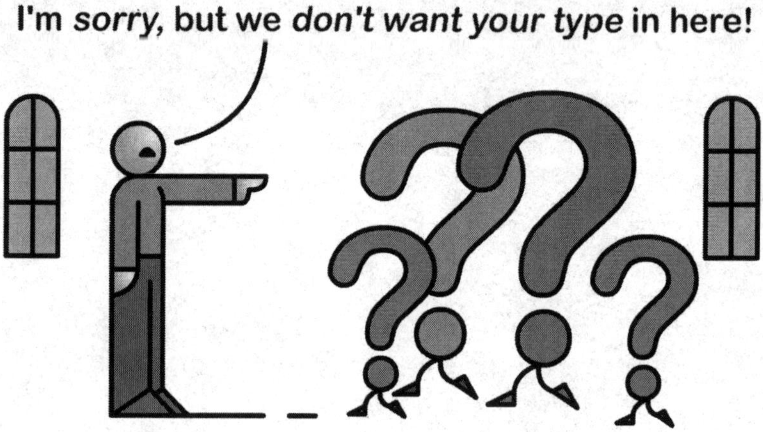
I'm *sorry*, but we *don't want your type* in here!

I would *like* to help, but my husband and I donate *all* our spare money to the cats and dogs home.

I'll have the 'Grace Meal' with a side of 'Wisdom Nuggets' and the 'Healing Power' soft drink please.
Fresh out, sir. But we do have '*Guilt* Burgers'.
DRIVE-IN McCHURCH

What's driving *you*?

I know *exactly* where I'm going...
I've been here *many* times before.
BLIND ALLEY

Ernie's 'spiritual/thinking' self was *so disgusted* with his 'fleshly/functional' self that he had to keep his head on a piece of string to save it from floating off in a *bid for freedom*.

"Do you want to live in eternity with *God*, or would you rather *burn* in *hell*?"

"*Why* would I want to live out an eternity with a 'god' like *that*?"

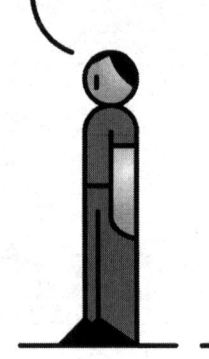

Climbing

the

sheer

hard

face

of

the

expectations

of

others...

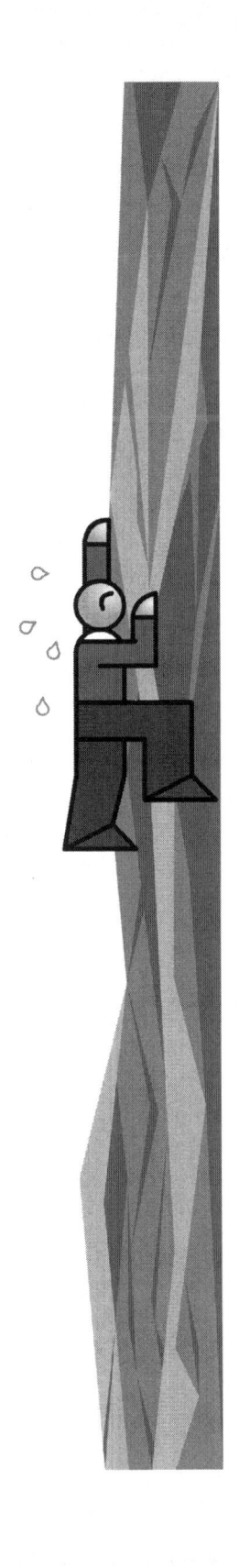

Faith and Doubt...
Perfect bedfellows.

I feel very comfy in mine.

I shoehorn mine in wherever I can.

I keep mine for special occasions.

I like to put mine on in private.

I like to show mine off.

I've outgrown mine.

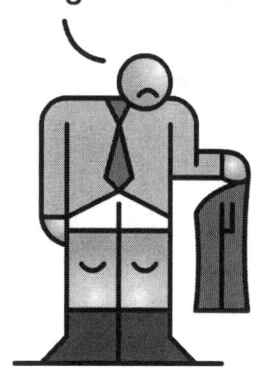

I like to run in mine.

I save mine for the weekends.

FAITH
How do *you* wear *yours*?

...In the name of JEEEEEYAYSUS!

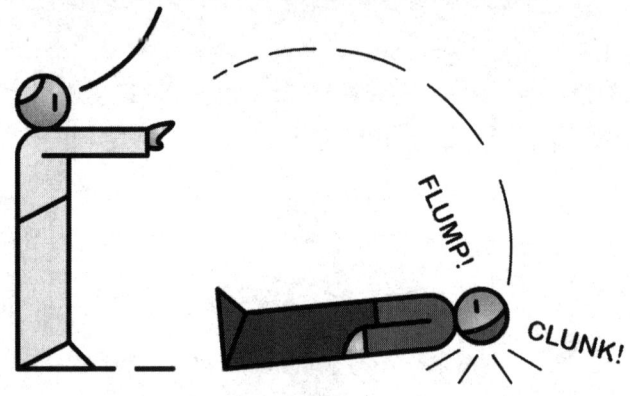

FLUMP!

CLUNK!

Did he *fall* or was he *pushed*?

Escapology eschatology = *bad* theology

Mum, Dad, I'm gay.
Oh thank goodness for that! Me and your father thought you were going to say that there was something *wrong* with you.
Family hug?

"The wind of the Spirit is *really* blowing through this place tonight!"

A faulty windsock.

...And this is
my *final* point...
PHEW!
PHEW!
PHEW!
PHEW!
PHEW!
PHEW!
PHEW!
PHEW!
PHEW!

I want to stand up for the oppressed... I want to love my neighbour... I want to fight poverty and injustice, so the world may know just how much God cares... I want to stand against governments who hold their people down and bring the light of God's love in to every aspect of this wonderful yet broken world.... And I want to do *all* this from my *bed.*

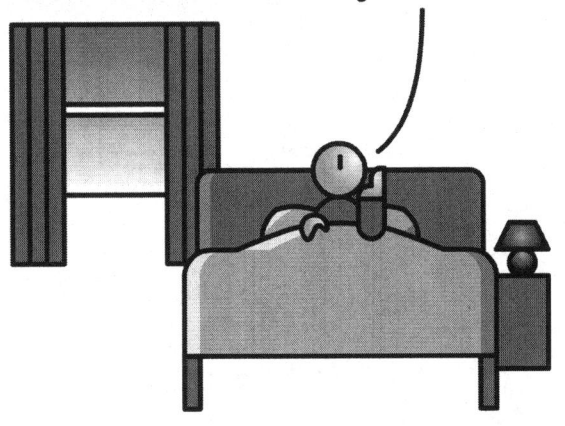

The daily grind of exercising faith is now a thing of the past with ASBO's all new...

FAITH REMOVAL SPRAY!

- Made from 100% CERTAINTY.
- No more suffering unwanted doubt.
- Wave goodbye to dispair.
- Say "hellooooo" to the new, less inquiring you.

ASBO... Making products because we care!

Caution: Too much exposure to certainty may render you useless to other people.

Middle class kids call it a 'gap year'.

"Have a great time."

Working class kids call it 'unemployed'.

"You need a job."

As the old saying goes...

E V GLICL1

"Give a man a fish and he'll stick it on the back of his car."

I will give my bounties to *no* man until I am *good* and *ready*.
Hi, babe.
OK, I'M *READY!*

When you pray, go to your room and close the door...

zzzZZzzzZzzZZZzzZZ

So Reverend... You'll marry us even though I've been married four times before?
Of *course* I will, my dear. God *loves* a 'trier'.

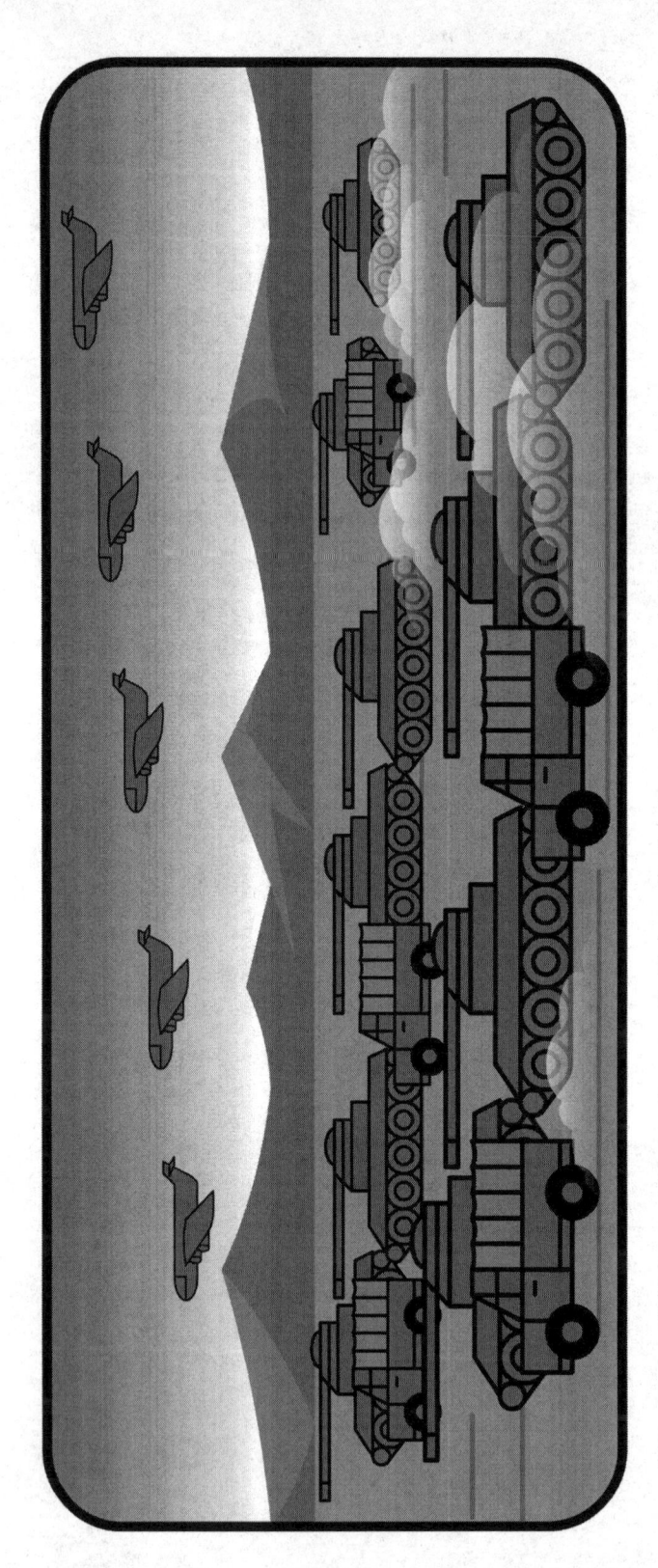

"Go into all the world and preach the good news to all creation."

This new God Nav is *brilliant!*
"At the next crossroads, turn right."
No way?! This is all *God Nav's* fault!

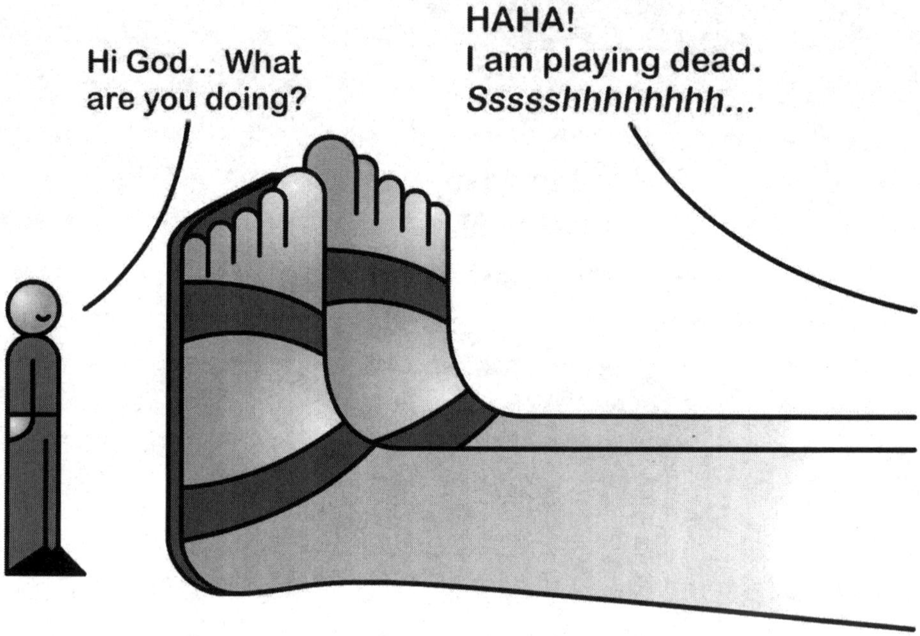
Hi God... What are you doing?
HAHA! I am playing dead. *Sssssshhhhhhh...*

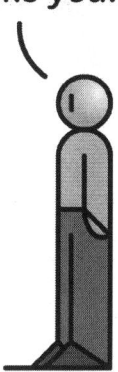

Hi... This is GOD TV. You know, I believe God is going to meet with us in a *really powerful* way today.

GOD TV

SPLAT!

God TV is brilliant today! Some foreign guy in a white robe and a beard has just come on and vandalised the set!

God is in my darkness.

You should feel *guilty* because you are a *sinner* and you're going *straight* to *Hell* for not accepting *everything* within this *great book!* You are *evil...* You *hear* me?.. *Evil!*

I said "do you have a 'gilt-edged' Bible?" *Not* a 'guilt-edged' Bible.

Jesus wants to heal you
of your terrible affliction.

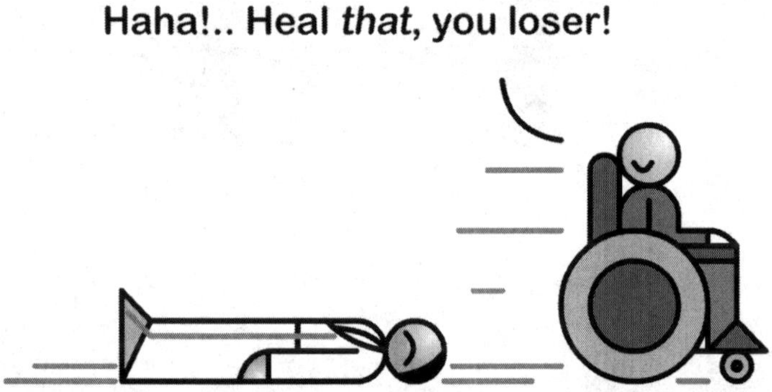
Haha!.. Heal *that*, you loser!

I have a *very* heavy heart.

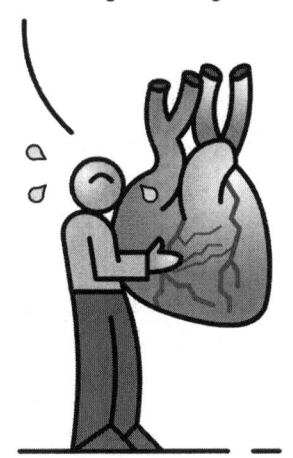

Come on out from behind there. It's *no* use *hiding*.

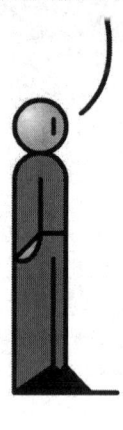

EXTRA BIG BIBLE

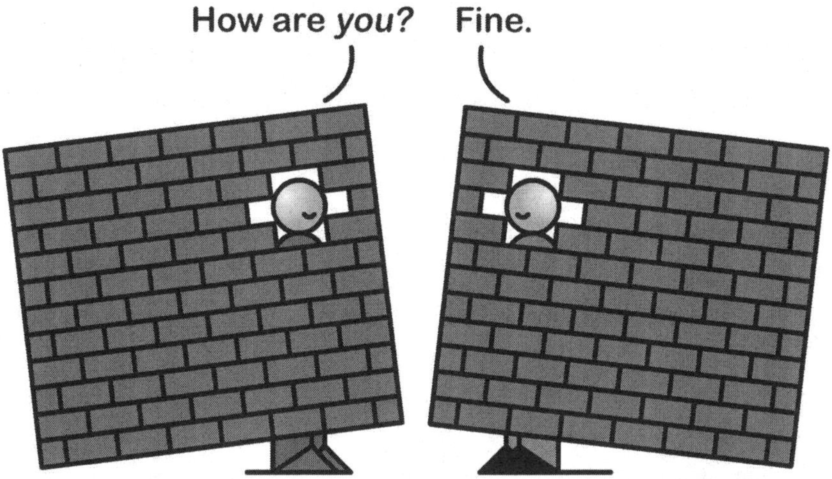
How are *you*?
Fine.

"I am just a computer made of meat."

"I am just a bunch of chemicals."

"I am just an idiot."

How do *you* devalue yourself?

ASBO'S ALL NEW...

GOD REDUCING MACHINE!

Reduce him down to size & pop him in your pocket!

- *With the new GRM you can make God just the size you need him.*
- *Making God smaller allows you to learn about him really fast.*
- *Impress your friends with your knowledge of him and boast to your friends and colleagues of the intimate relationship you and God have.*
- *No one need ever find out just how small your God is... It will be our little secret.*

ASBO... MAKING FAITH EASIER!

During the service I had a mild panic attack, a heart murmur, self-doubt leading to a moment of depression and a headache throughout. After the service, not *one person* asked me how *I was*.

My theological education *didn't* come *cheap.* So it's *important* I tell *everyone,* as *often* as I can, how *much* I *know.*

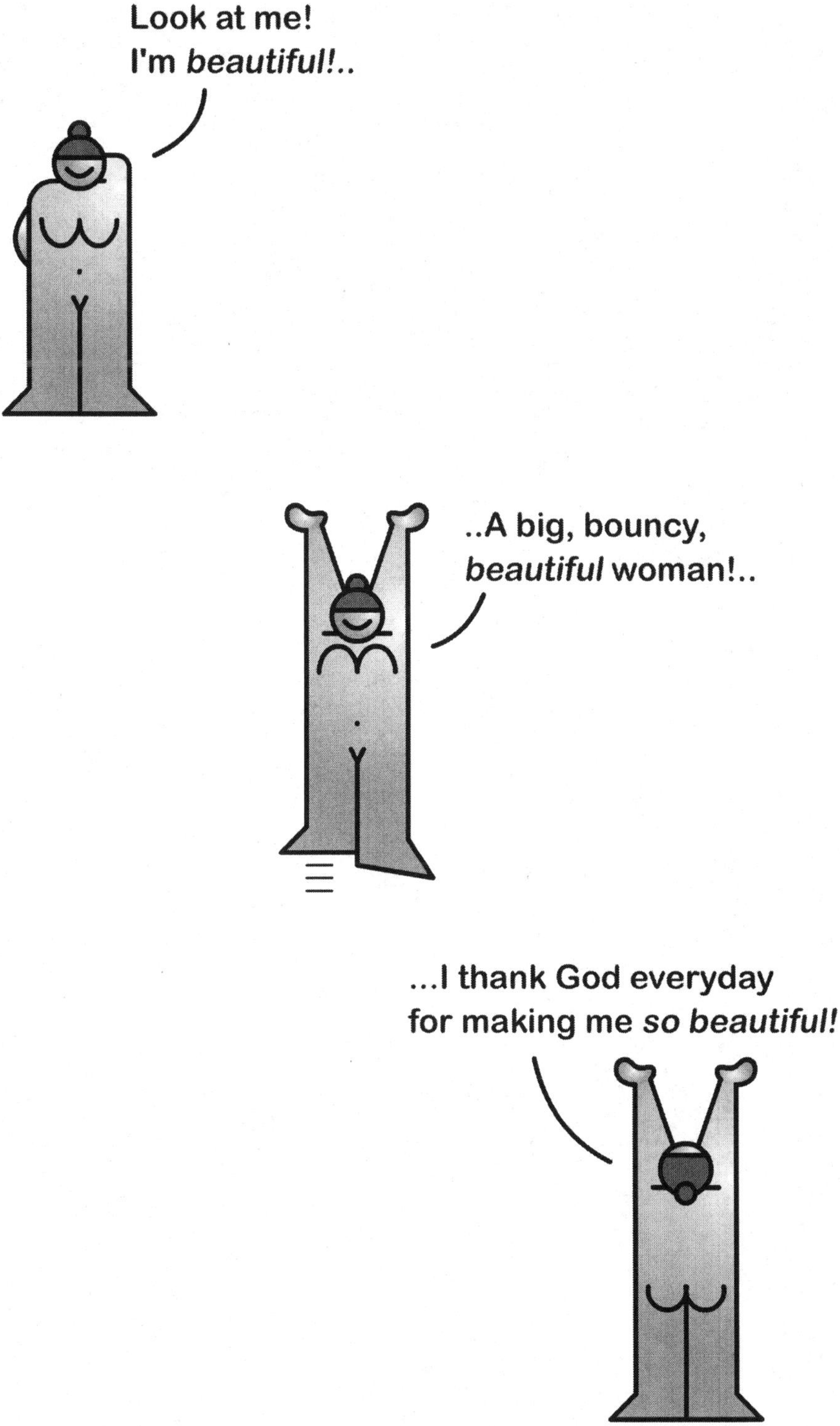
Look at me!
I'm *beautiful!..*
..A big, bouncy,
beautiful woman!..
...I thank God everyday
for making me *so beautiful!*

ASBO is proud to introduce...

GOD'S EARPIECE!

"**WOW!** It's just like listening to the radio!"

- Hear the voice of the Creator loud and clear.
- Judge people and tell them what to do with complete confidence.
- Now you will always have an answer when you need one.
- No more need for endless soul searching.
- You'll have absolute certainty 24/7!

YOU CAN BE SURE WITH ASBO!

Caution: Some people think hearing voices is strange. Now you can tell them how wrong they are.

When I see the suffering in the world, the poverty, the sickness, the hunger, the war, the environment treated with such a lack of respect and the greed that seems to have swallowed so many... I could cry for a thousand years.

Man... You could really use *Jesus* in your life.

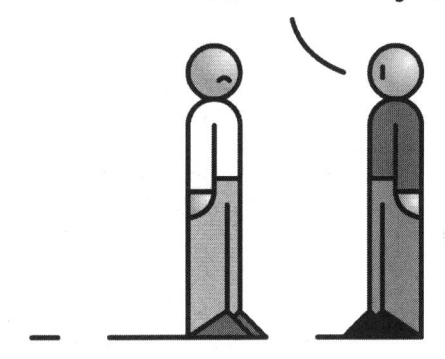

I *AM* Jesus!

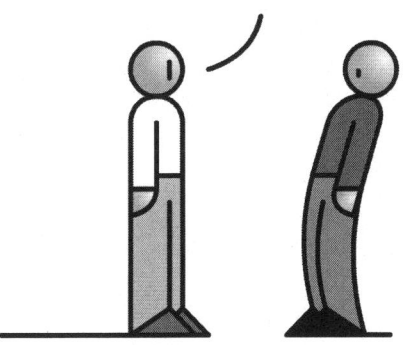

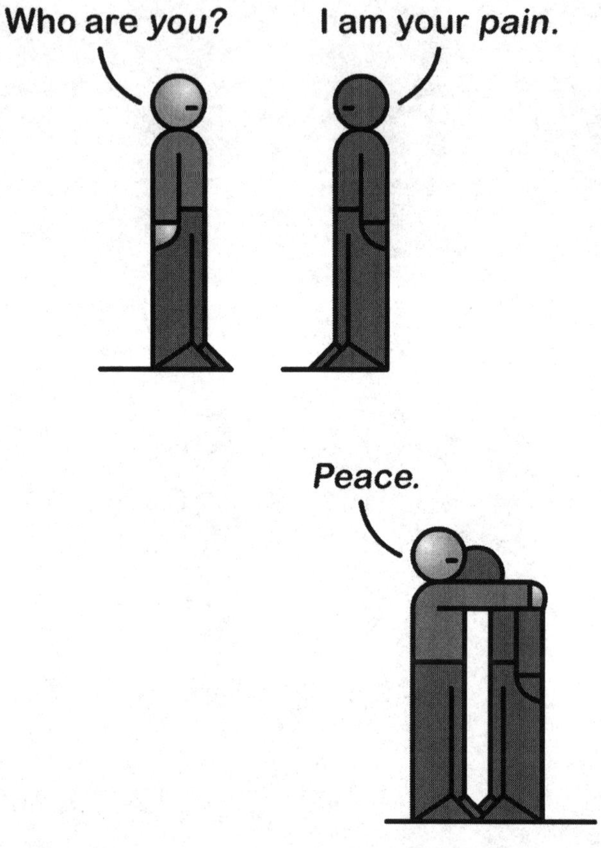
Who are *you*?
I am your *pain*.
Peace.

Yes, of course I love the church...
It's the *people* I can't stand!

You need to be 'fully in the river!'
You need to be 'aflame!'
You need to be 'swept away in the tsunami of God's overwhelming love!'
I need new friends.

I'm *scared.*

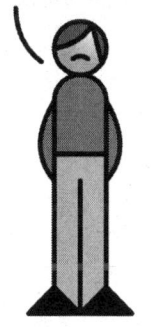

Perfect love casts out all fear,
perfect love casts out all fear,
perfect love casts out all fear,
perfect love casts out all fear,
perfect love casts out all fear,
perfect love...

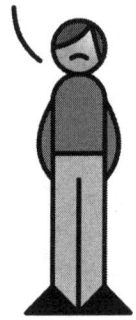

I'm *still* scared.

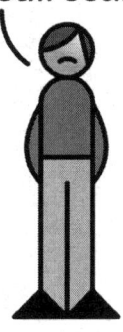

Brought to you by ASBO...

GROW YOUR OWN RELIGION!

GROW YOUR OWN RELIGION

INCLUDES THE POPULAR PARTS OF:

BUDDHISM
CHRISTIANITY
ISLAM
HINDUISM
& MUCH MORE!

To save you the effort, we have taken a seed from here and a seed from there and planted them in an ill-prepared mulch to create the perfect, inoffensive religion.
All you have to do is let it grow.
You won't even have to worship!

ASBO... Making life less taxing!

Warning: Your religion may look a little limp. Don't worry, this is normal.

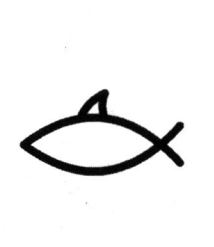

MALE   FEMALE   MALE / FEMALE

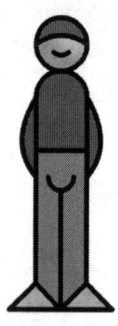

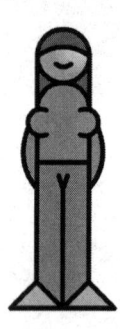

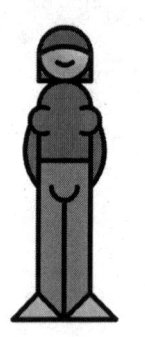

All made in the image of God.

I'm having an identity crisis. I don't know who I am anymore.
Don't look at *me.* *I'm* in the *same boat.*

So sad to see you here again.
I'm addicted to the institution.
H.M.PRISON

So great to see you here again.
I'm addicted to the institution.
ALL SAINT'S

It is not what you think, say, blog, tweet, sermonise or put in your manifesto that shows me what you believe...
It is what you *do*.

Many wildlife experts say that homosexual behaviour is widespread amongst certain primates.

You can keep your mitre on.

We need to put *Jesus* back in to the centre of *all* aspects of our relationship.

Hmmm... I'm not *sure* I'm *comfortable* with this.

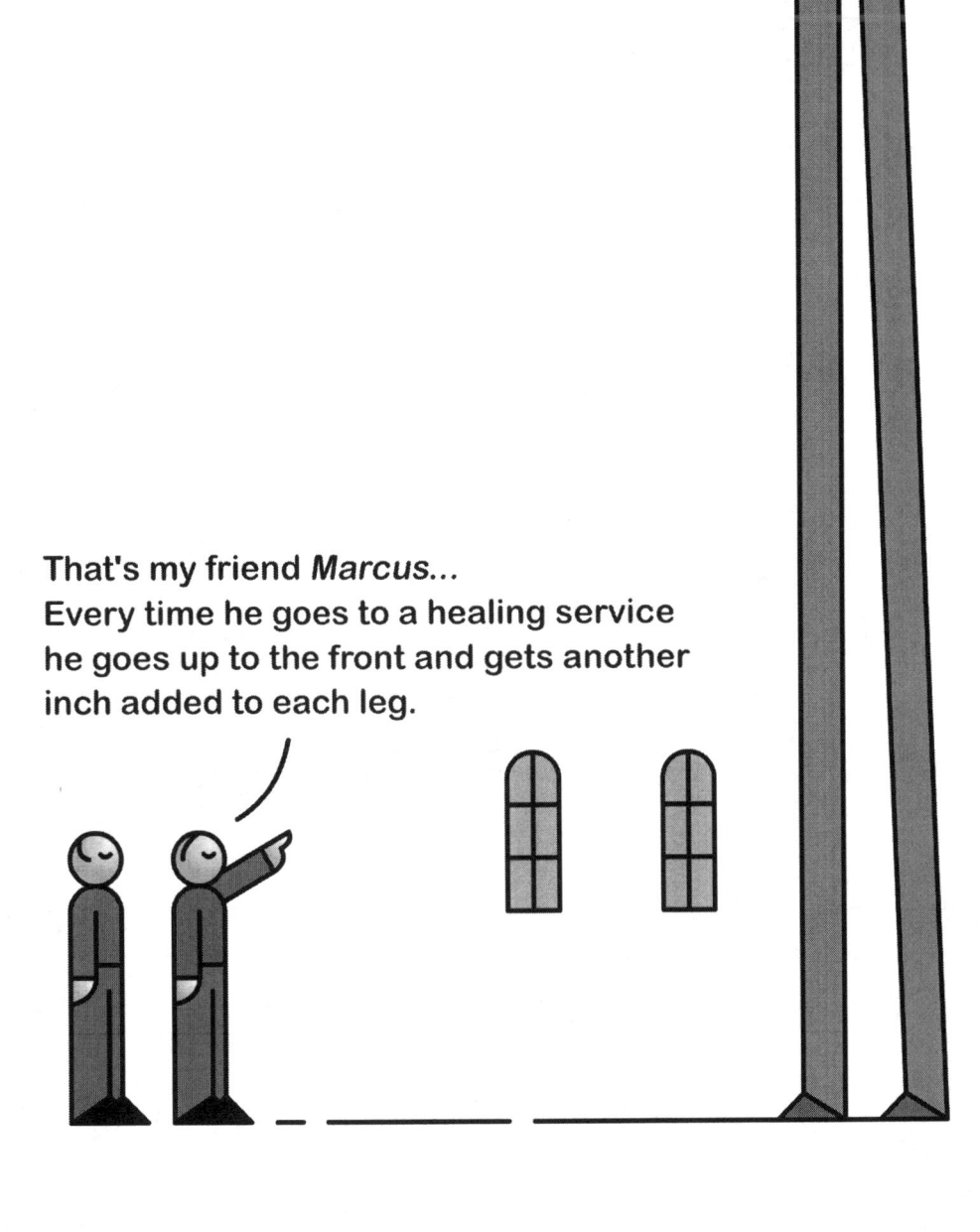

That's my friend *Marcus*...
Every time he goes to a healing service he goes up to the front and gets another inch added to each leg.

Good news... I've just discovered I have a couple of *hours spare.*
!
That *is* good news... Let's have a *meeting.*

So, if it came down to it... would you switch off my life support machine?
Of *course*... It would be my *absolute pleasure,* darling.
!

ASBO is proud to introduce...
GOD'S MOUTHPIECE!

- *With this little beauty you will be able to speak with complete authority about things you know nothing about.*
- *No one will be able to argue with you as you share your wisdom.*
- *Watch your friends gasp in awe and shrink under the weight of your 'oh so wise' judgements and pronouncements.*
- *With God's Mouthpiece you are sure to become the centre of attention... Just what you always craved!*

Warning: You will lose friends if used excessively... But at least you will know that you were right!

ASBO... COMMITTED TO MAKING YOU FEEL SPECIAL!

I believe in the local church.
Mine is *only* nine miles away.

Father, I have sinned. I've thought about doing it with my neighbour's wife.
To *think* about doing it is as much a sin as *actually* doing it, my son.
So... You're telling me I might as well have *done it?!*

LOVE IS GOOD!

Rebuke, rebuke, rebuke.
Rebuke, rebuke, rebuke.
Rebuke, rebuke, rebuke.
Ooh, I do *so love* rebuking.

A man on his way to church to meet a woman.

Marriage...

Names: Brian & Irene
Wedding: Church
Together: 7 years

Names: Adam & Steve
Wedding: No
Together: 23 years

Names: James & Kay
Wedding: No
Together: 11 years

Names: Kath & Jane
Wedding: Civil ceremony
Together: 4 years

Men are *not* from Mars.

Man ——
—— Martian

Women are *not* from Venus.

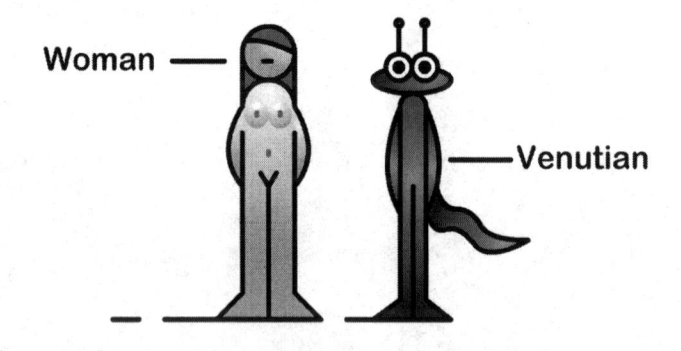

Woman ——
—— Venutian

Darling... I thought you said you'd mend the toilet!
Proverbs 27... 'A nagging wife is like a dripping tap!'

Your job is to find different ways of saying the same thing week after week.

MINISTER SCHOOL

Mr. Happy goes to church.

10am

12pm

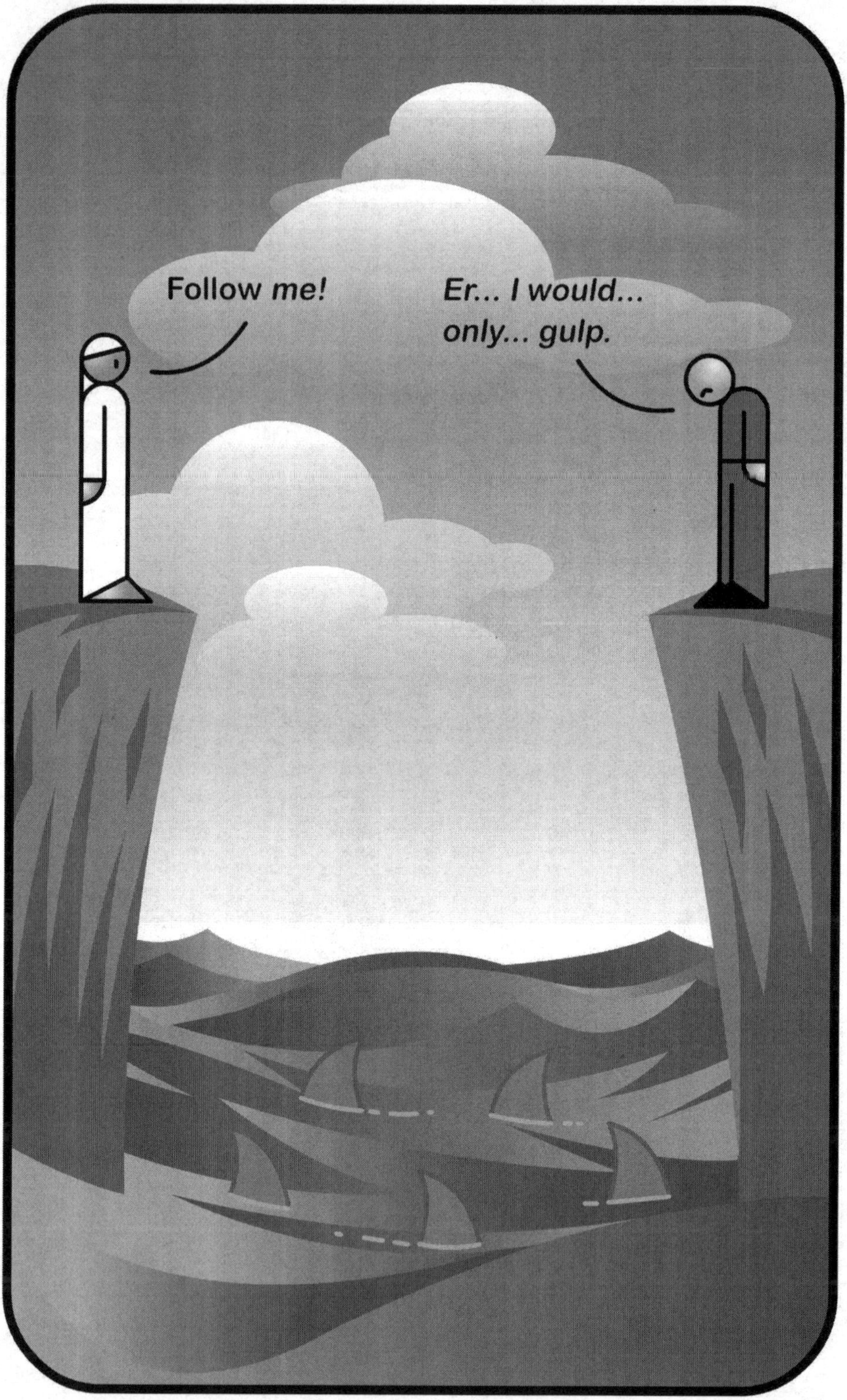
Follow *me!*
Er... I would... only... gulp.

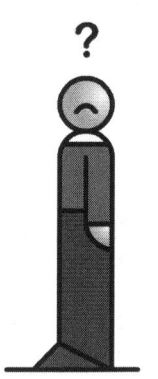

My husband *left* me.   **I don't *blame* him.**

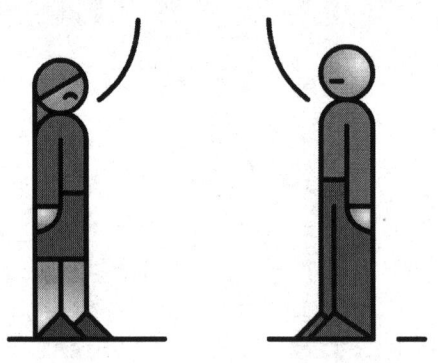

Things you're not *allowed* to say
but would dearly *love* to.

I'm angry about the state of the world! I'm angry about war, violence, greed, racism, sexism, the banks, the government, the opposition, tax evasion, homelessness, spam, call centres, the Daily Mail, global warming, insurance companies, the cult of celebrity, David Cameron, Tony Blair, the price of a pint, being told how to live my life by rich film and rock stars, Simon Cowell, conservative evangelicalism, junk mail, dried fruit, the public transport system, the BNP, poverty, homophobia, cancer, gossip, adversarial know-it-alls and much, much more!

But mostly I'm angry about my own weakness in the face of it all and angry about my own part in it.

Aah believe that God told Adam to name all the animals.
That there's a 'buffalo'.
BANG!
That there's a 'bear'.
BANG!
That there's an 'unbeliever'.
BANG!

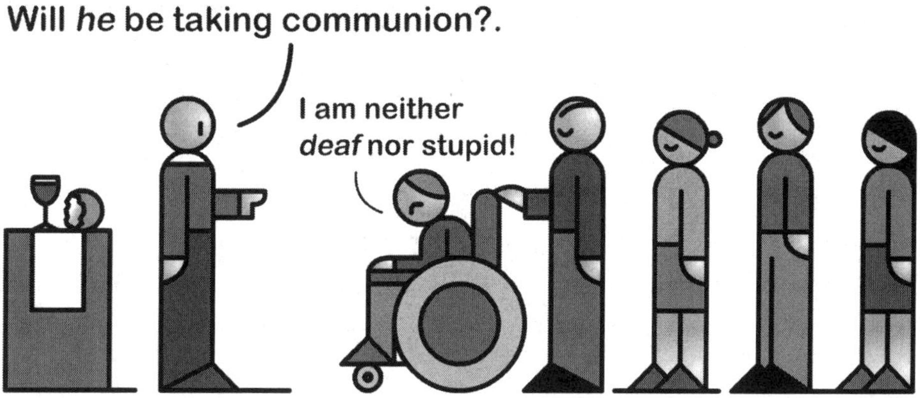
Will *he* be taking communion?.
I am neither *deaf* nor stupid!

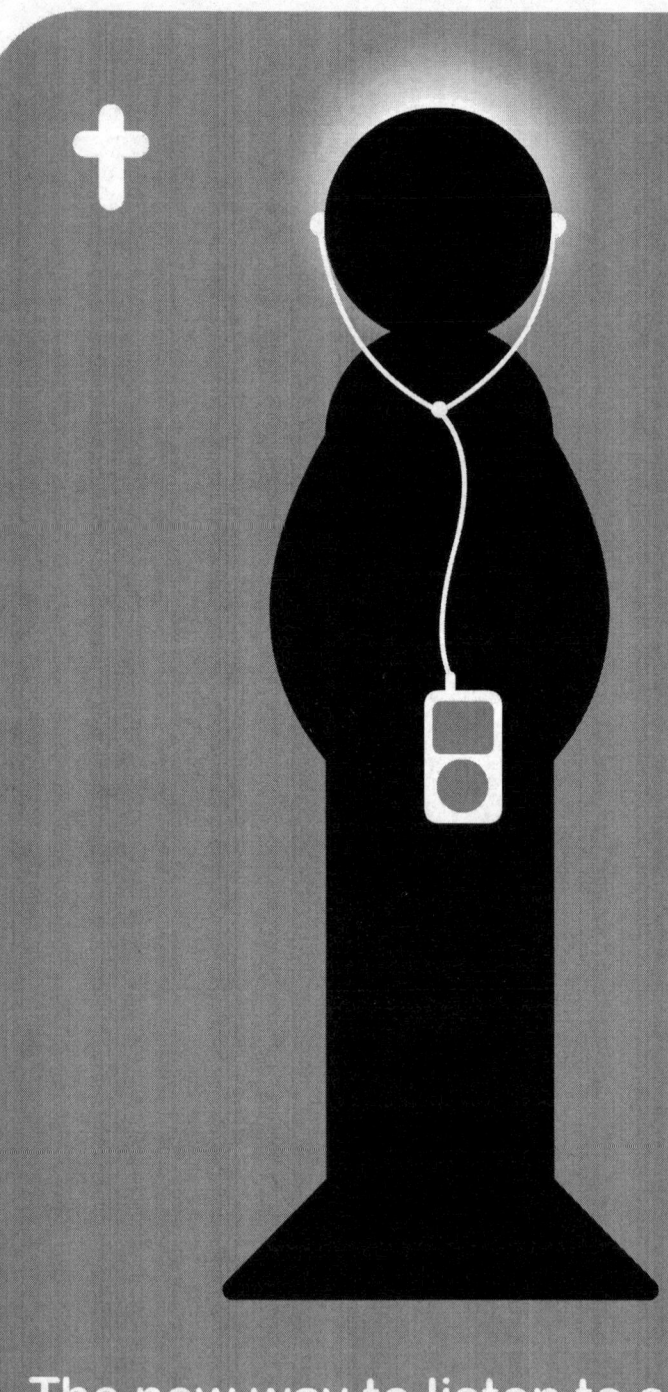

The new way to listen to sermons

Alright, alright! I now *definitely* believe *everything* you tell me to! You were *right* and I was *wrong* all along! I can see it now. I *promise*, I'll *never* think for myself again... *ever!*

I'm normally an optimist, but I have to admit, regarding this one issue in my life, I have no hope at all.

In the year 2020 AD all the churches in the world mysteriously blew up.

By the year 2025 AD the Christian people had forgotten that they once owned buildings and their numbers were added to daily.

Two Christians from AD30 are sucked into a time vortex which transports them to AD2011...

What, *no* women bishops?!
ARE YOU *BACKWARDS*?!!

Father, I have sinned. Yesterday I found myself wanting to kill someone.
To *think* about doing it is as much a sin as *actually* doing it, my son.
Hmmm... Not *quite* as bad though, eh?!

Yes, I *know* he's the *King of Kings,* but he's just *not* the man I thought he was!
MARRIAGE GUIDANCE

I no longer believe in *'virtual* reality'.
Real people, *real* opinions, *real* emotions, *real* shopping, *real* relationships, *real* junk mail, *real* joy, *real* sadness, *real* empathy, *real* crime, *real* porn, *real* info, *real* poetry, *real* art, *real* cruelty, *real* goodness, *real* truth, *real* lies, and so it goes on...
There is nothing *'virtual'* about it *at all*.

I don't understand. One moment he was *on fire*, the next he'd *burnt out*.

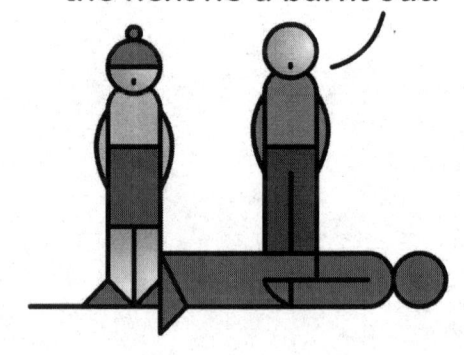

✝

Before iTunes
Before the iPod
Before the iPhone
Before the iPad
Even before
iLife itself...

iAm

The average parish pecking order...

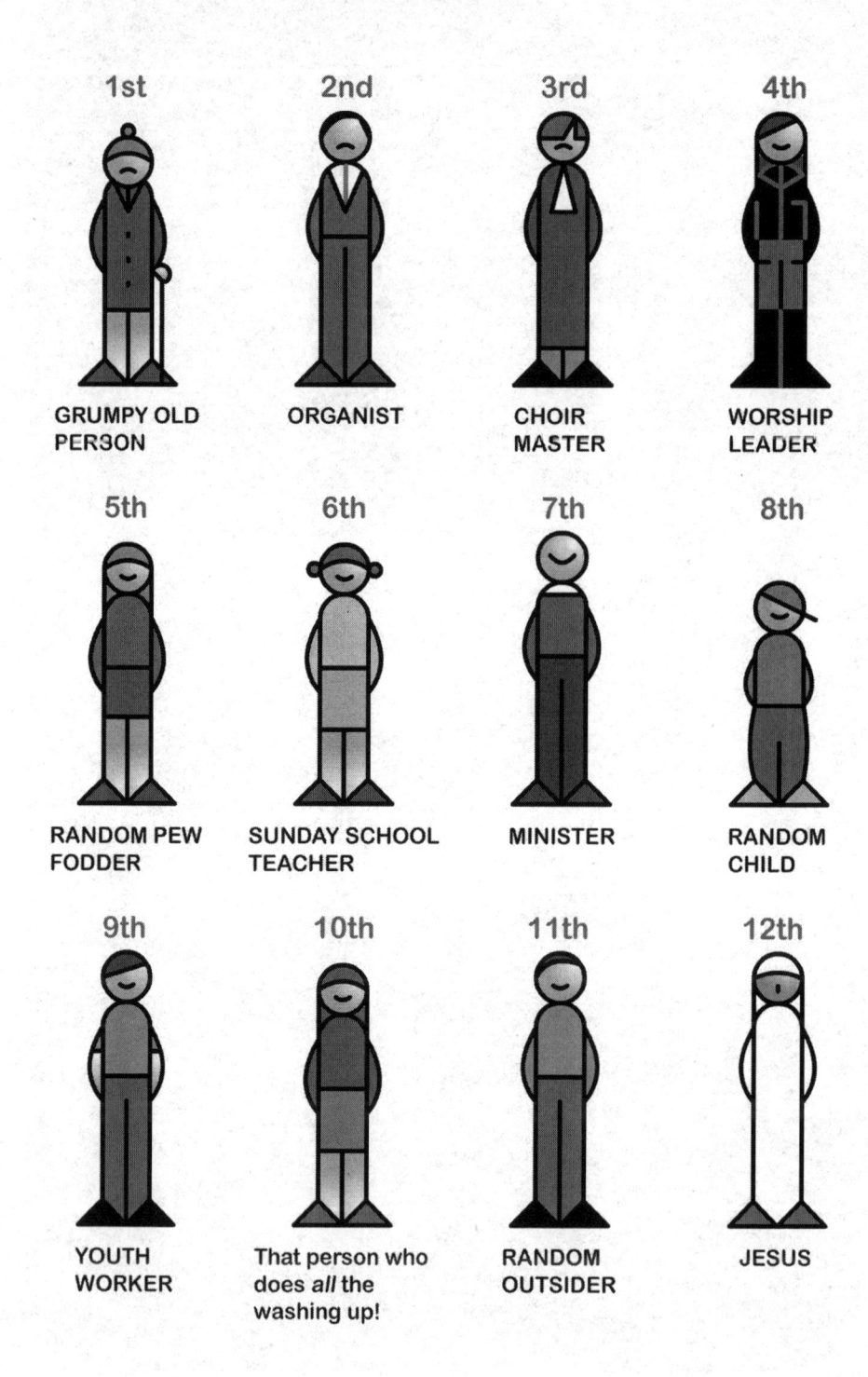

1st — GRUMPY OLD PERSON
2nd — ORGANIST
3rd — CHOIR MASTER
4th — WORSHIP LEADER
5th — RANDOM PEW FODDER
6th — SUNDAY SCHOOL TEACHER
7th — MINISTER
8th — RANDOM CHILD
9th — YOUTH WORKER
10th — That person who does *all* the washing up!
11th — RANDOM OUTSIDER
12th — JESUS

You have a *very* large building... You must have an *enormous* congregation.
No... It's just that the pastor's head got *so* big we had to *rebuild* the church to accomodate it.

The pastor is having time away with Elsie, his wife.

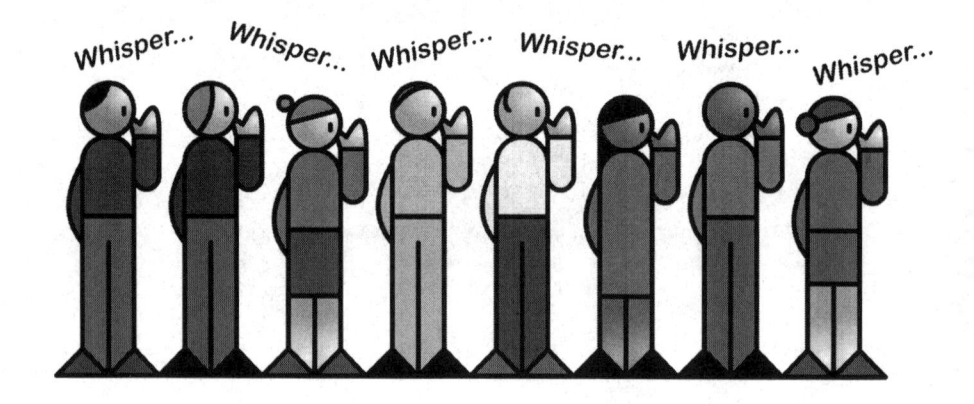

Whisper... Whisper... Whisper... Whisper... Whisper...

Whisper... Whisper... Whisper... Whisper... Whisper... Whisper...

The pastor is having it away with someone else's wife!

Whisper... Whisper... Whisper... Whisper... Whisper...

Pie chart church...

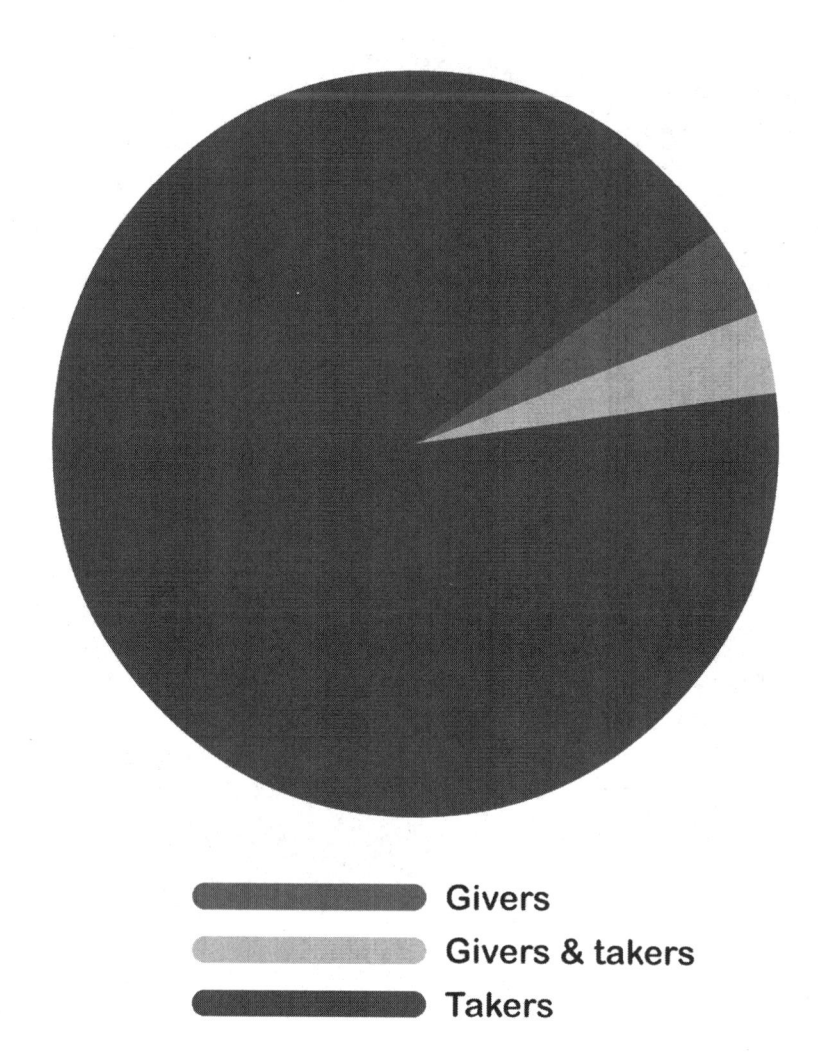

- Givers
- Givers & takers
- Takers

Things die when you pin them down...

...Or else they were already dead.

Okay... We've fed, clothed and sheltered you, now *pleeeeease* come to our church.

?

Classical is the *only* music with any *real* merit...
The poor are *lazy*... My Jimmy's *top* of his class...
They should *lock them up* and *throw away* the key...

POP!

Pomposity *must* be pricked.

THE BEST WORSHIP ALBUM IN THE WORLD... EVER!

PRAISE HIM on the KITCHEN SINK!

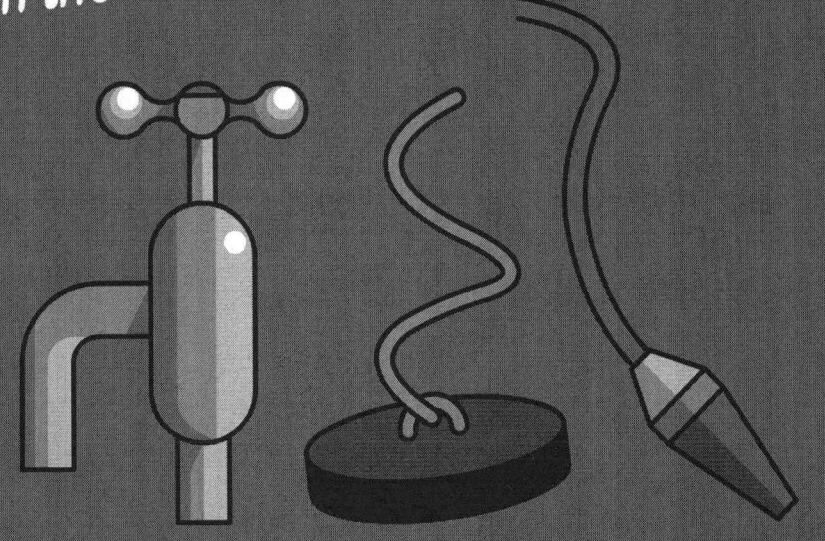

Featuring
RED MANMATT on PLUG
KENNY GRAHAM on TAPS
& TOM CHRISLIN on SHOWER HOSE.

Brought to you by *NO INTEGRITY MUSIC*, a branch of *ASBO...*
SELLING MUSIC THE WORLD DOESN'T NEED!

Dear Lord, *Please* may the weather *stay* like this for the *whole* holiday. Amen.

Hmmm...

I am so *blessed*, because *God* has chosen *ME* to bring good news to sinners *everywhere*, and he's chosen *ME* as a living *witness* to his divine *light.*

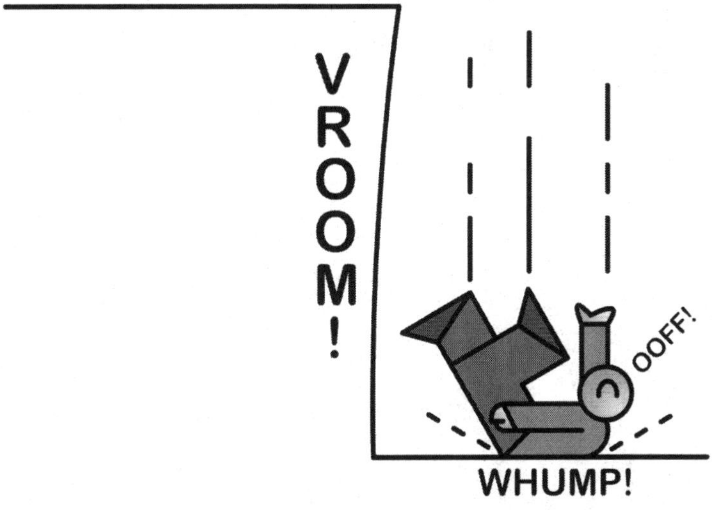
VROOM!
OOFF!
WHUMP!

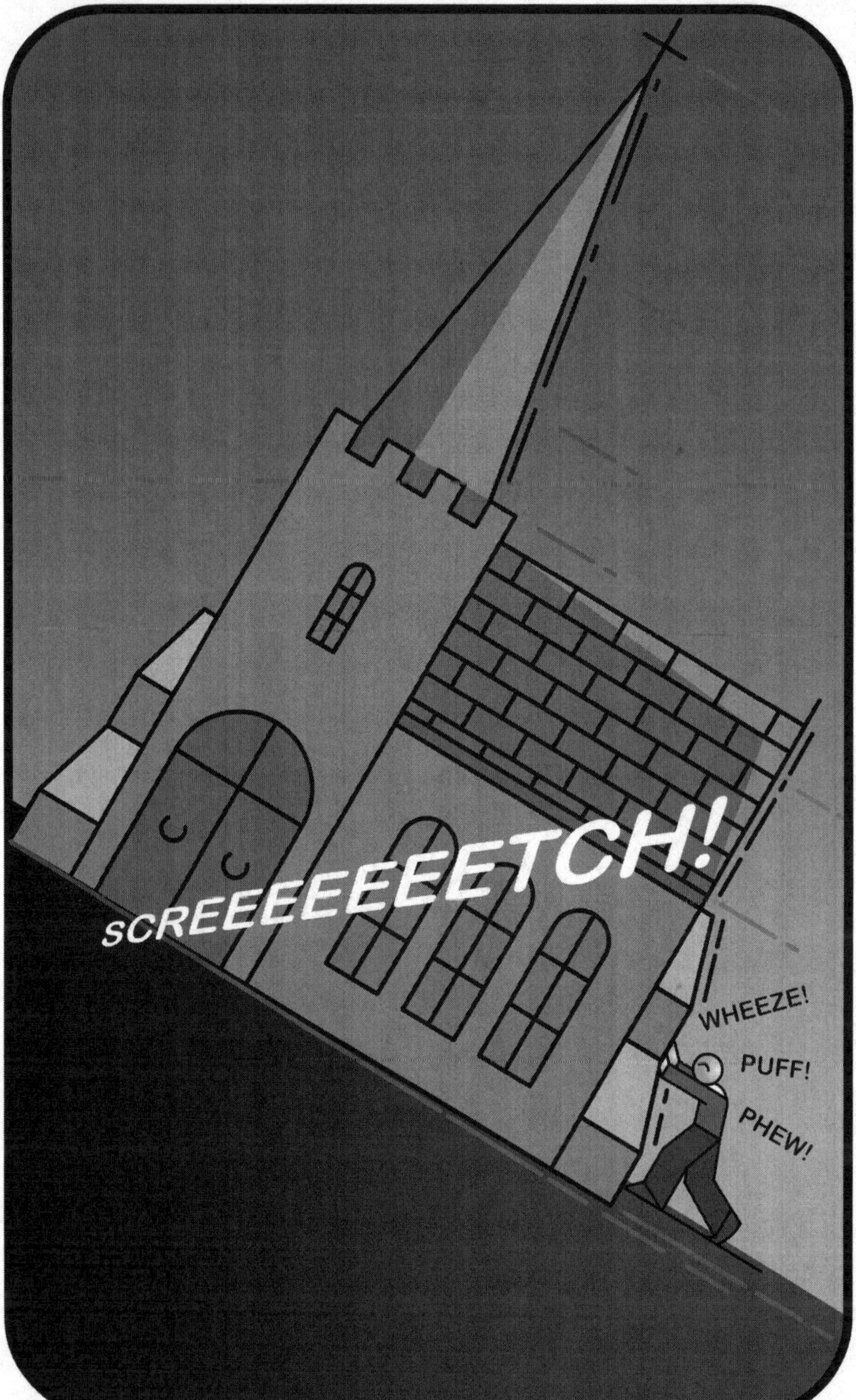
SCREEEEEEEEETCH!
WHEEZE!
PUFF!
PHEW!

Let's just have a moment of quiet reflection.

SCREAM!
BAWL!
WAAAGH!
BANG!
CRASH!
Mutter... mutter... mutter...

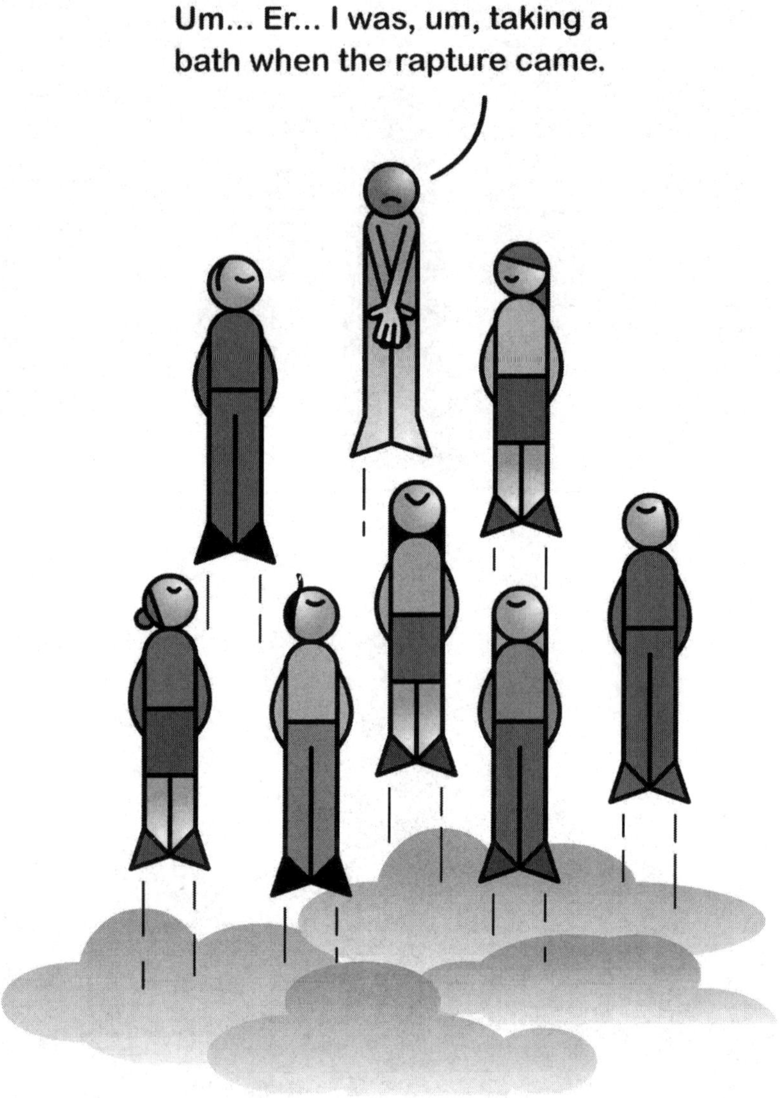
Um... Er... I was, um, taking a bath when the rapture came.

We'd like to start up a youth club.

Good idea! We'll need to set up checks with the CRB. We have to make sure we have the correct insurance... Ooh, we ought to look in to Health and Safety and make sure we have the right claim forms and get the parents to sign a disclaimer form etc...

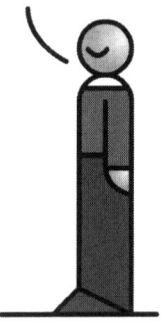

ZZZZZZZZZ
ZZZZZZZZZ
ZZZZZZZZZ
Thank you for such a *wonderfully* refreshing service.

Darling... Isn't it time you came to bed?!
Proverbs 21... 'Better to sleep on the roof than live with a nagging wife!'

I've worked in the third world, in war zones, nursing the injured and the poor.

I've worked on a checkout all my life.

Saints occupy all walks of life.

Honestly... The amount of times I've heard the *same old quotes* and the *same old sermon...*

Yeh, you'd think the Bible was only *fifty pages long!*

I *didn't* know you were going to bring me to a *science fiction* convention.

Actually, this is a gathering of the *Christian* denominations and they *all* come from *completely* different planets.

PUZZLE PAGE

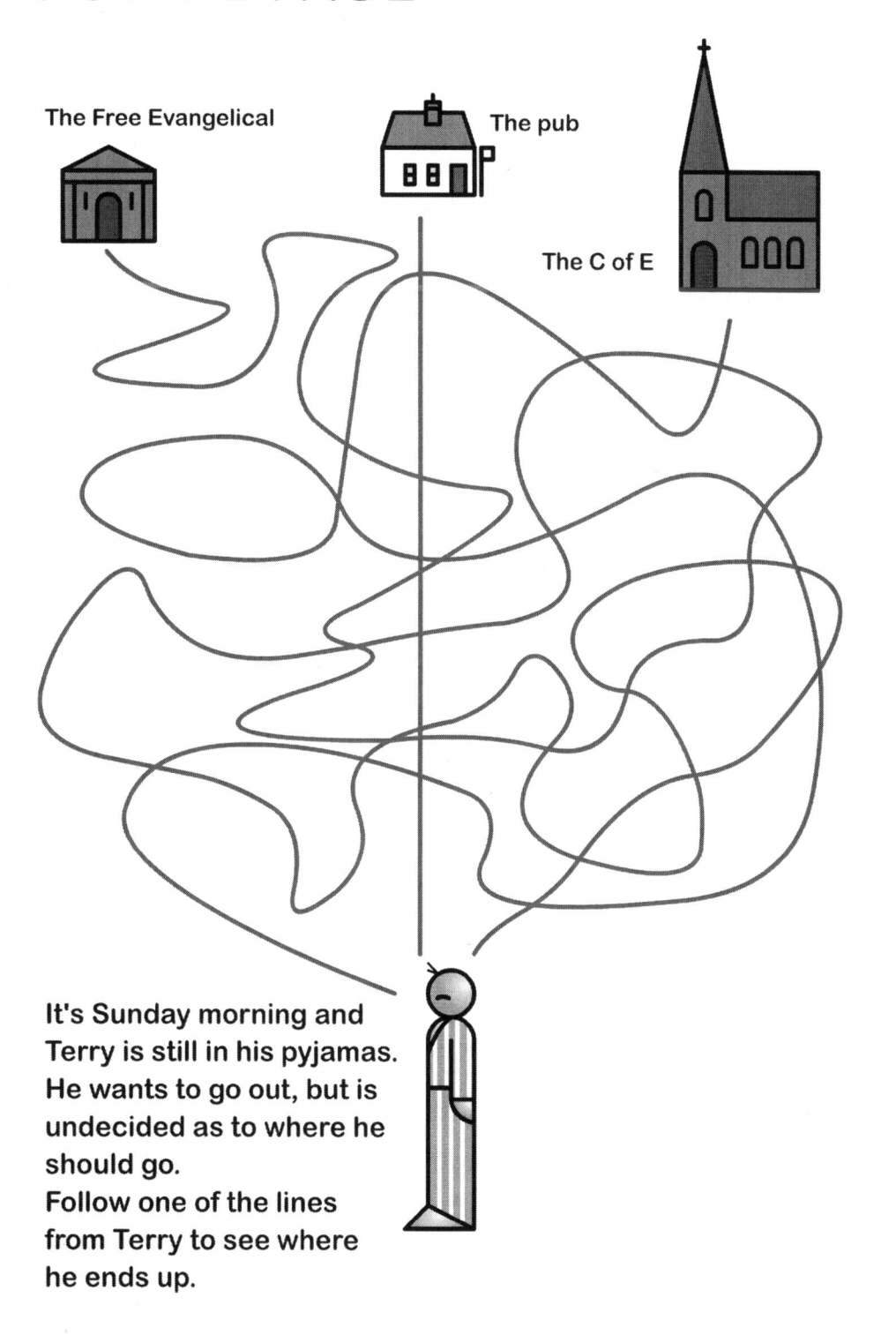

The Free Evangelical

The pub

The C of E

It's Sunday morning and Terry is still in his pyjamas. He wants to go out, but is undecided as to where he should go.
Follow one of the lines from Terry to see where he ends up.

"Mirror, mirror…"

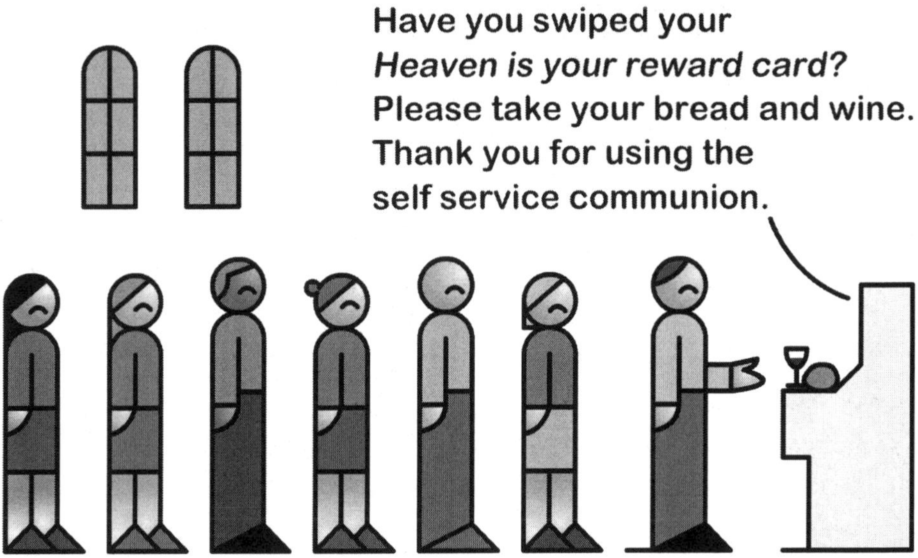
Have you swiped your *Heaven is your reward card?* Please take your bread and wine. Thank you for using the self service communion.

This is Sharon, your new bishop. Unless you don't want her, which is fine by us.

Equality... but only if you *want* it.

I'm not happy in large groups, don't like singing and I'm not too keen on lectures. Hmmm, I wonder if I should go to church in the morning.

I empathised once... Entered into another man's experience of life... I didn't like it... I'll not be doing *that* again in a hurry!

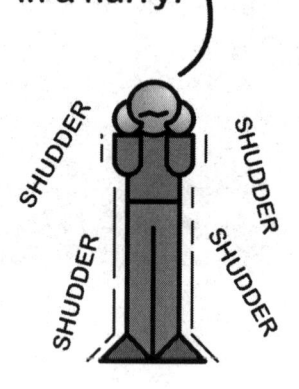

SHUDDER SHUDDER SHUDDER SHUDDER

New from ASBO...

Sin Detection specs!

- *See the darkness and the sin in the lives of those around you.*
- *Embarrass friends by revealing them for who they truly are.*
- *Name and shame sinners with relish and abandon all day long.*
- *Force the world in to becoming more honest... More like you.*

WITH ASBO'S SDS EYE ACCESSORIES YOU WILL ALWAYS BE ONE STEP AHEAD!

ASBO... YOUR FRIEND IN A FALLEN WORLD.

My father left home on my eleventh birthday,
my mother beat me with a big stick everyday,
my uncle was always trying it on with me,
my sister went off with my husband,
my brother is in prison for murder,
my daughter is a crack addict,
my son is in debt to a loan shark
and my doctor has given me five days to live...
So I'm feeling a bit depressed.

Hmmm... You need to *snap out of it.*

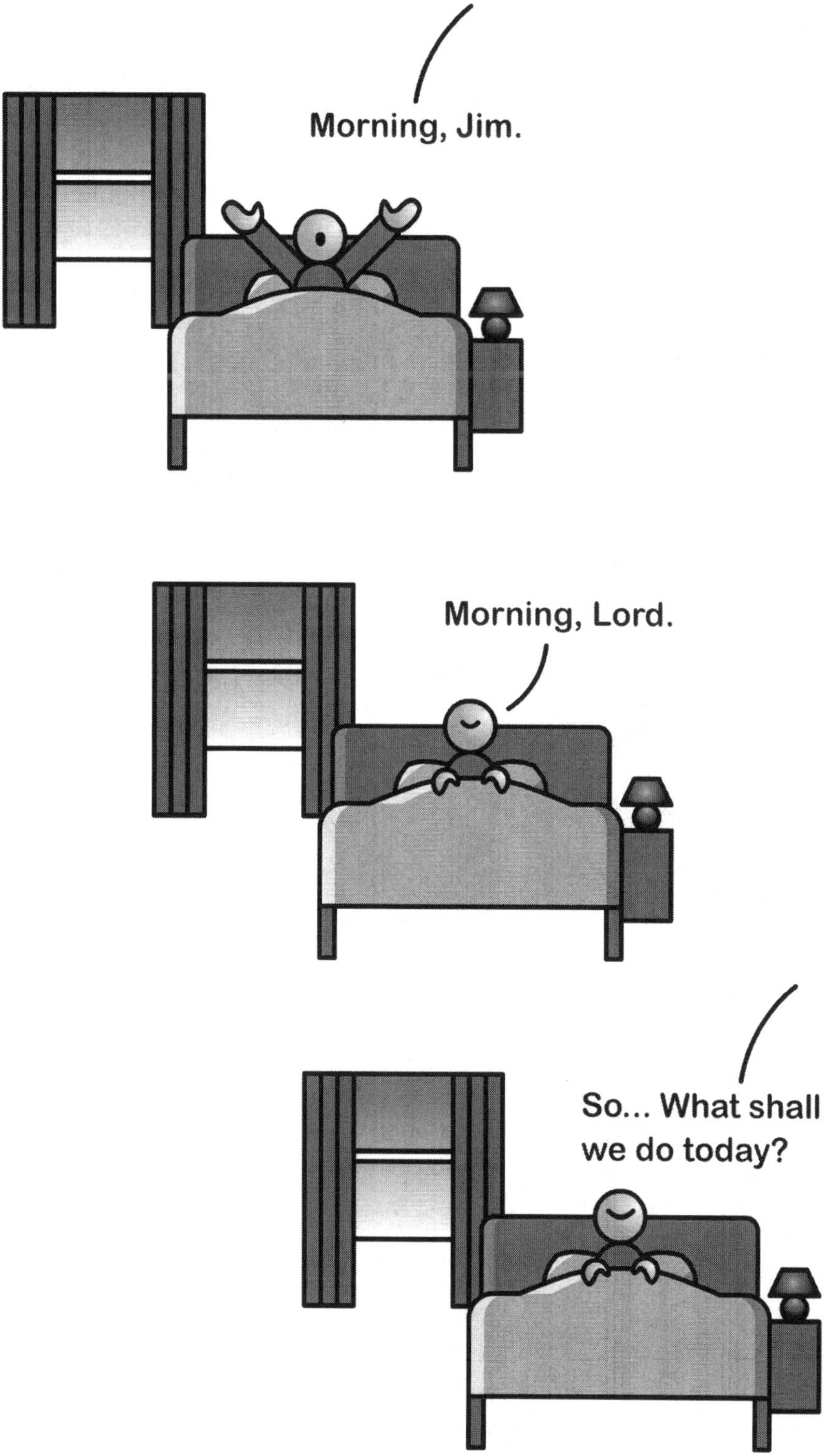
Morning, Jim.
Morning, Lord.
So... What shall we do today?

Sweety... There's someone on the doorstep who needs our *help!*
Darling... *Can't* you see I'm *busy* reading my *book*, entitled 'How To Be A Better Christian?!!

There is *no* God. Just as there is *no* spaghetti monster in the sky!

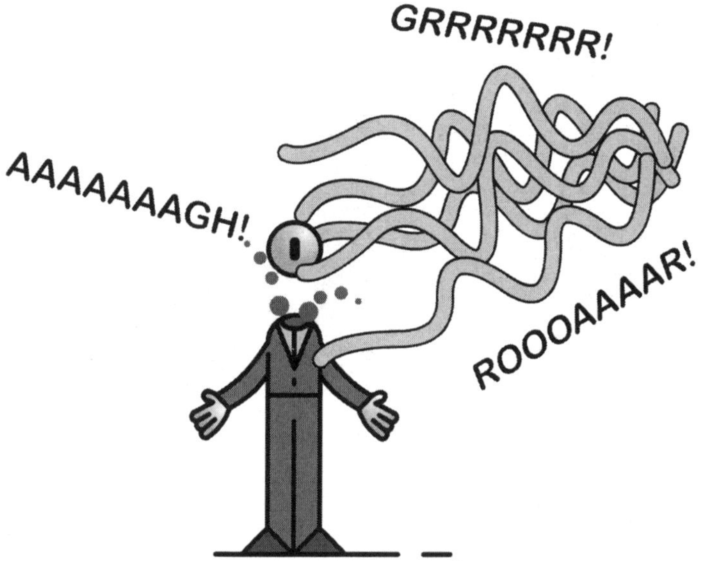
GRRRRRRR!
AAAAAAAAGH!
ROOOAAAAR!

I always feel better having spent a bit of time with him.

Wouldn't it be neat if all the malicious gossips spontaneously combusted!?

PUZZLE PAGE

Spot the self harmer...

The people below are all different ages and from very different backfrounds, professions and beliefs. Which of them do *you* think self harms?

It could be anyone.

The Greed Creed

I believe in Greed, the Market Almighty,
the Creator of Money,
and in the Profiteer, His only Son, our Lord:

Who was conceived of the Capitalist,
born of the Free Market Economy,
suffered under His own pompous piracy,
crucified Himself, died, and was buried.

We descended into recession.

The third day He arose again from the dead.

He ascended into Hedge Funds
and sits at the right hand of Greed the Market Almighty,
whence He shall come to fleece the living and the dead.

I believe in Banks, the Holy Catholic Bank,
the communion of bankers,
the covering over of their sins,
the resurrection of the economy,
and riches everlasting.

Amen.

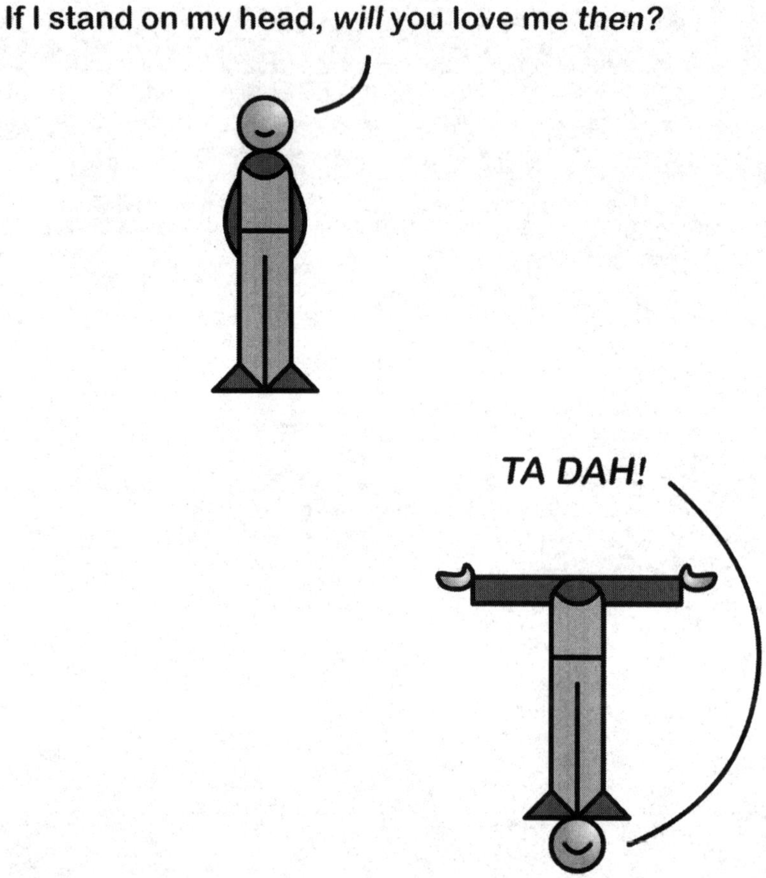
If I stand on my head, *will* you love me *then*?
TA DAH!

Leave me alone... I've made my decision and I'm staying *here... forever!*

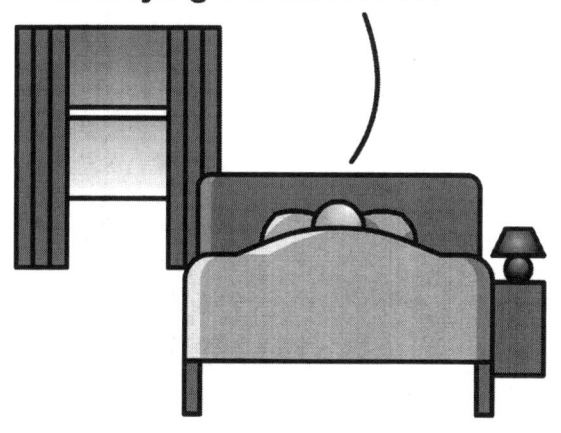

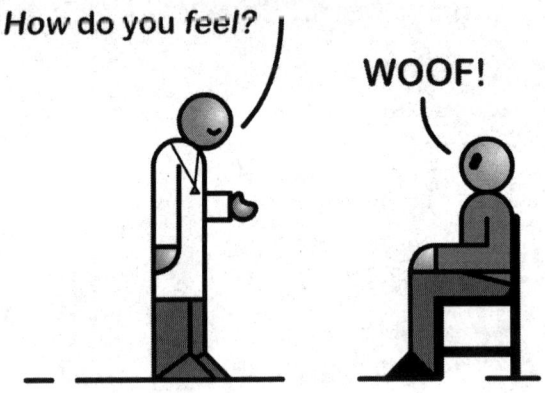

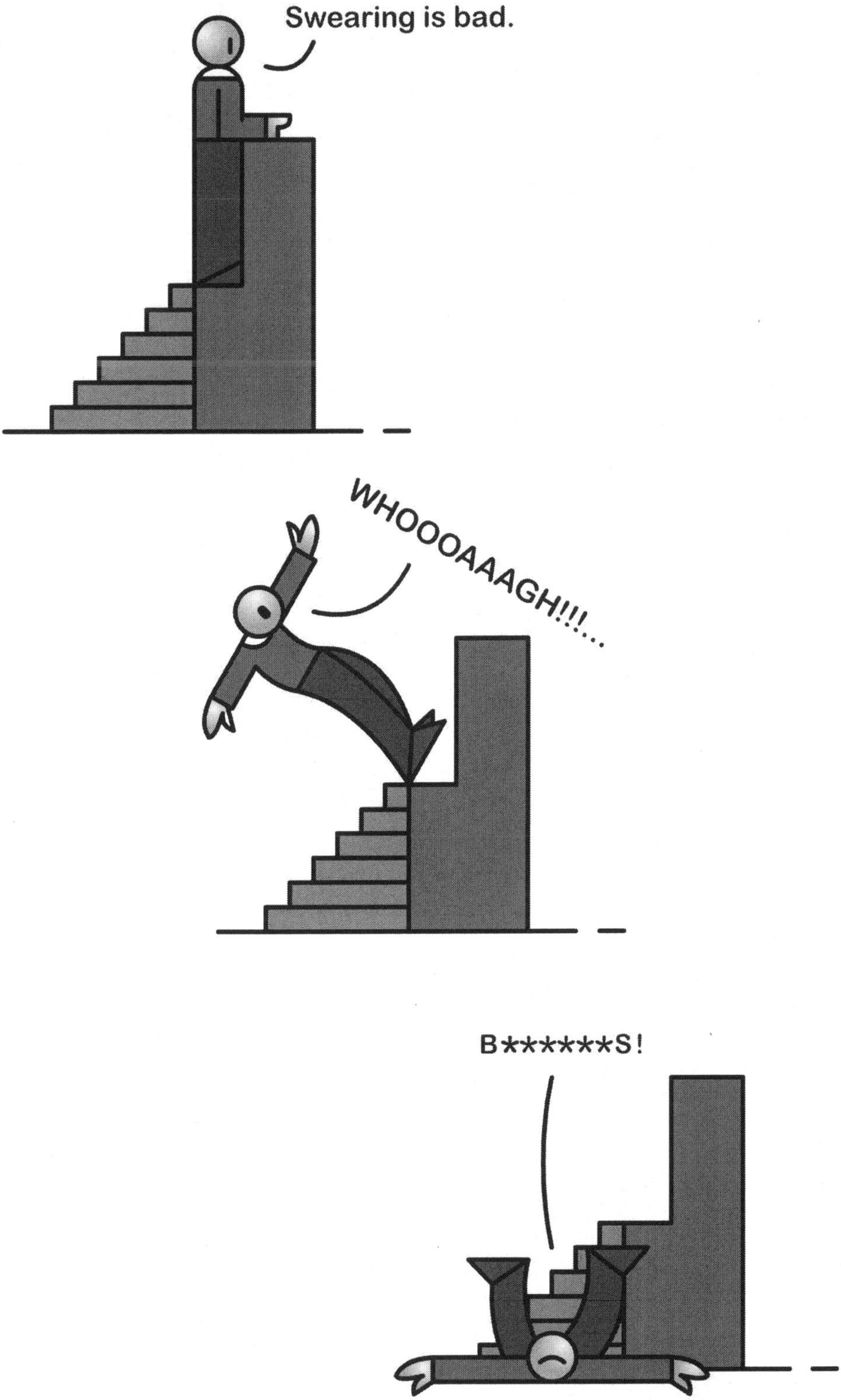
Swearing is bad.
WHOOOAAAGH!!!...
B******S!

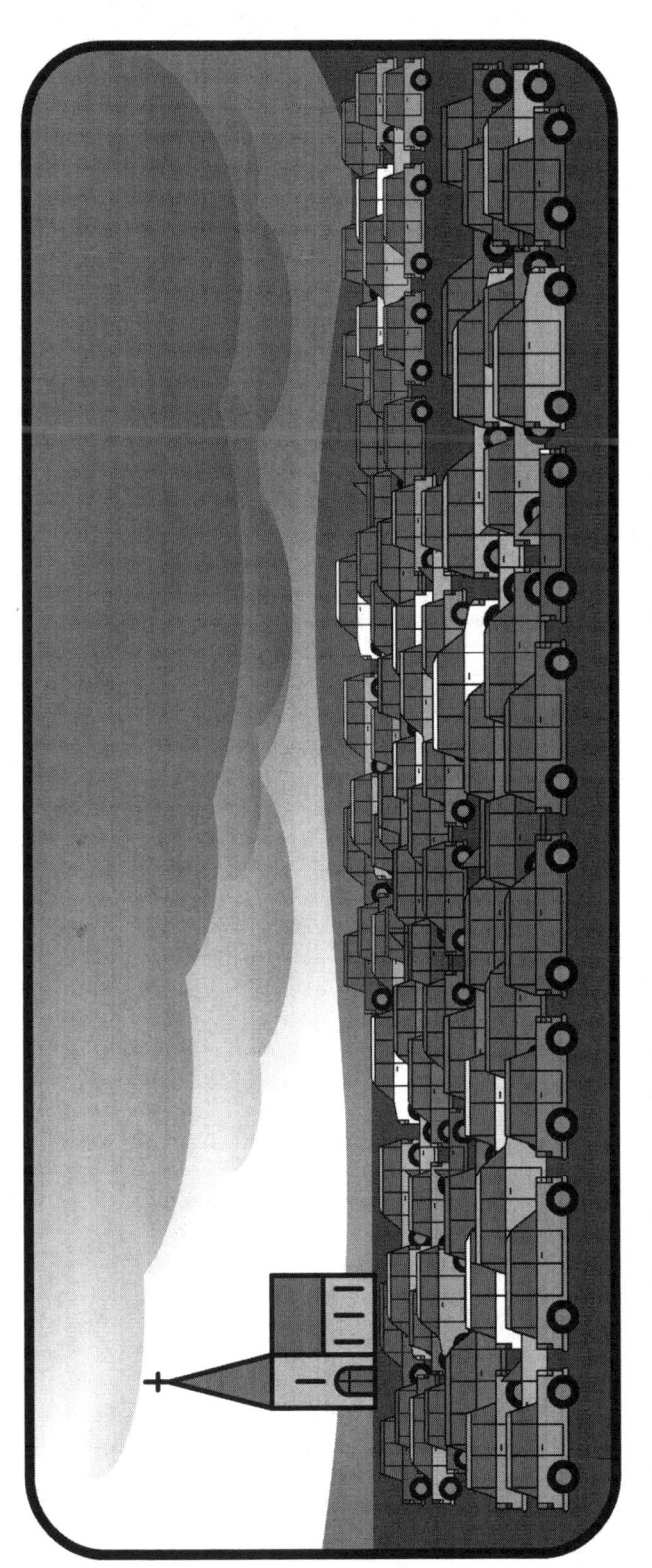

The congregation turn up to hear a wonderful sermon on the environment.

Today I'm going to teach you how to run away, how to be non-communicative and how to suppress your feelings.
Thanks, Dad.

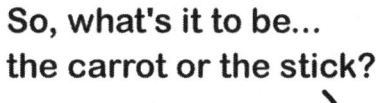

Our church is *brilliant!* Big, strong and problem *free!*

I hate *everything* about the way I am.

But you're *wonderful,* cool, sexy *and smart.*

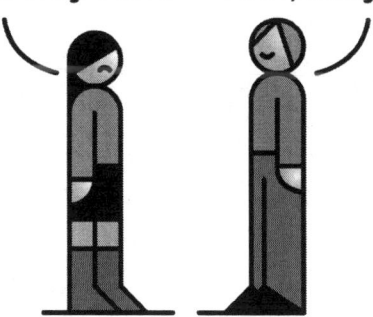

Wow! He thinks I'm wonderful, cool, sexy and smart!

You *don't* have to *raise* the dead to bring the *dead* back to *life.*

The Devil in the dock.

> It wasn't *me!*.. It was *you* and your *stupid* human nature!.. That's right, *YOU!* I wasn't even *there!*.. I'm *not* omnipresent, you silly little person! I was doing *other stuff* at the time! Take responsibility for your *own* actions and STOP BLAMING ME! Honestly, *humans!*.. I don't know *why* God bothers!

Hey *brother*... I'd like to *speak* the *truth* to you in *love*.
Okay, just give me *one* minute.
One minute later...
...I'm *ready!*

PUZZLE PAGE

Which of these characters is thinking outside the box?

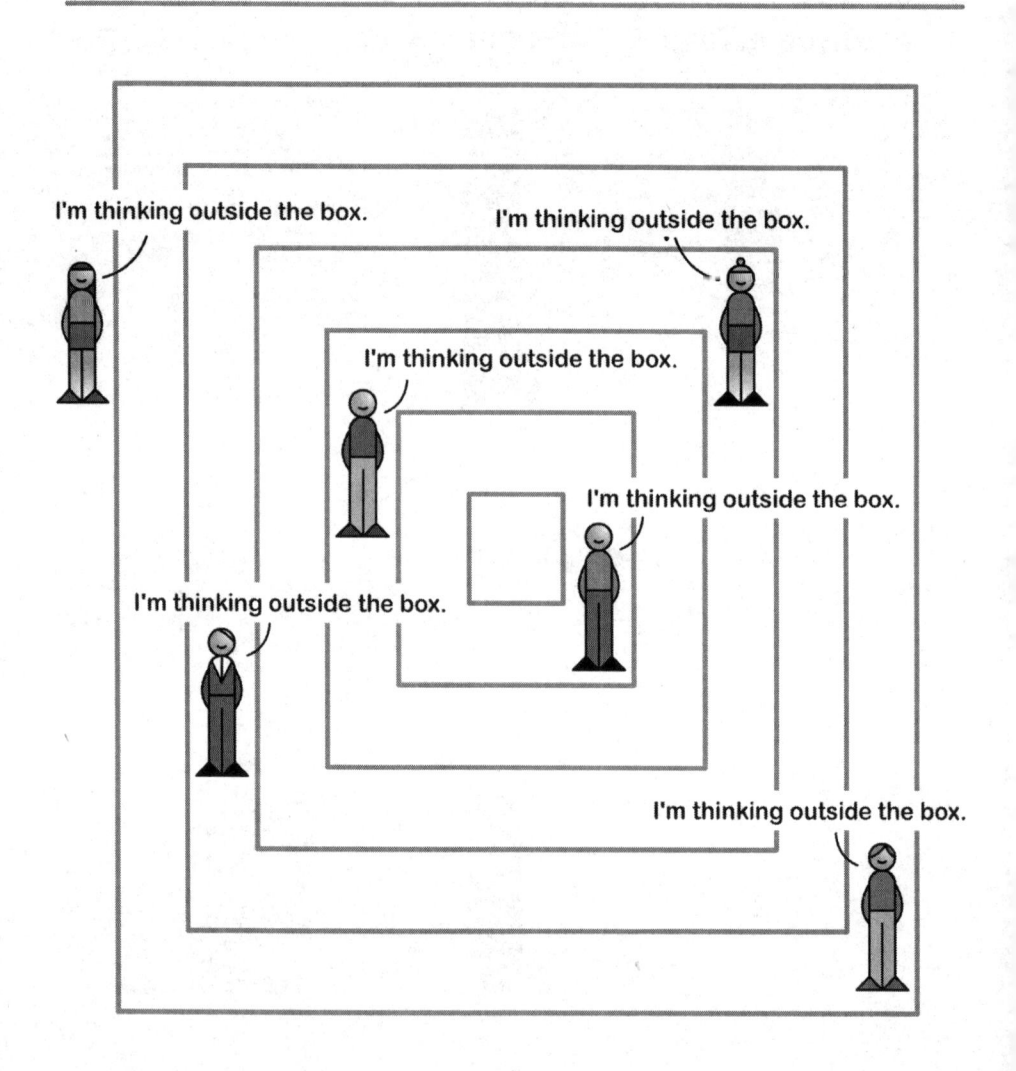

- I'm thinking outside the box.
- I'm thinking outside the box.
- I'm thinking outside the box.
- I'm thinking outside the box.
- I'm thinking outside the box.
- I'm thinking outside the box.

None of them.

It's *not* what *I* think that's important...
It's *not* what *you* think that's important...
It is what *God* thinks that *truly* matters...
And *this* is what *God* thinks!

PUZZLE PAGE

Can you answer these 3 simple questions?

Who am I?

Where do I come from?

Where am I going?

No one answer is correct.

Too *busy* to marvel...

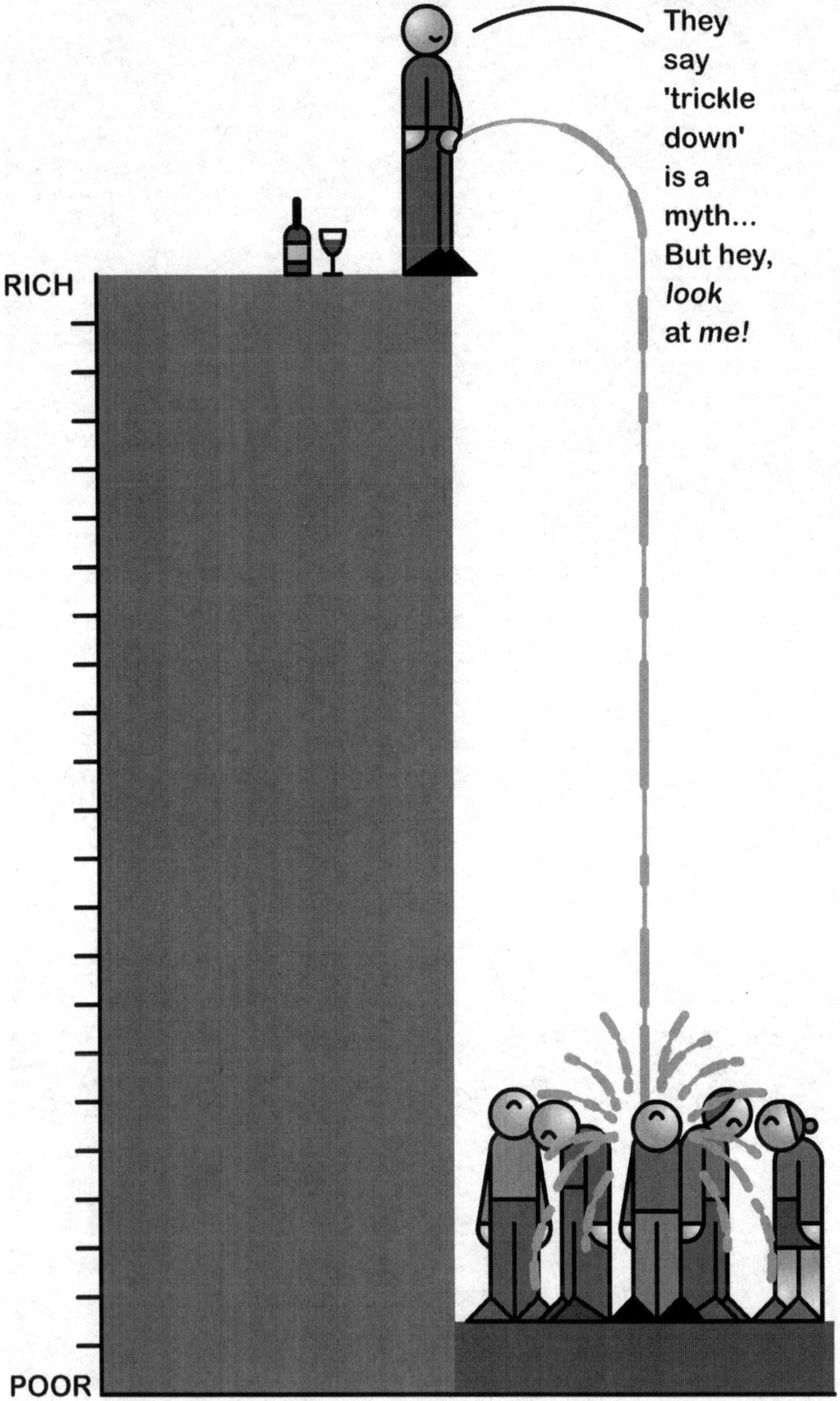

They say 'trickle down' is a myth... But hey, *look* at *me!*
RICH
POOR

God's Kingdom is upside down.

It's not YOUR church!
You DON'T have to DO EVERYTHING!
You CAN relinquish control!
You DO NOT have to be *all* things to *all* people!
You CANNOT POSSIBLY have ALL the answers!

Sigh...
Vicar deprogramming is a *very* lengthy business.

Vicar's wife syndrome.

I *do* have a *proper* name you know!
I actually have a *higher* IQ than *he* does!
His last *three* sermons were *my* idea!
I *don't* just make *cakes*!
He only became a vicar because *I* said he'd be good at it!

I am a person in my *own* right!
I have written *several* books, you know!
All his *best* ideas are *my* ideas!
I went to bible school too *and* got *better* grades than him!
I don't just do *knitting*!

'VIRGO.
This week, take long walks and get out and about. Breathe in the fresh country air. This will be beneficial to your health and give you the chance to meet new and interesting people. It's time to shake a leg, get active and try something new.'

What my minister calls his *'vision'*
I think of as *'our imprisonment'*.

I'm a broken hippo and I spend all my days wallowing.
I'm a hippo who's been hurt...
...but I will *not* let 'wallowing' define me.

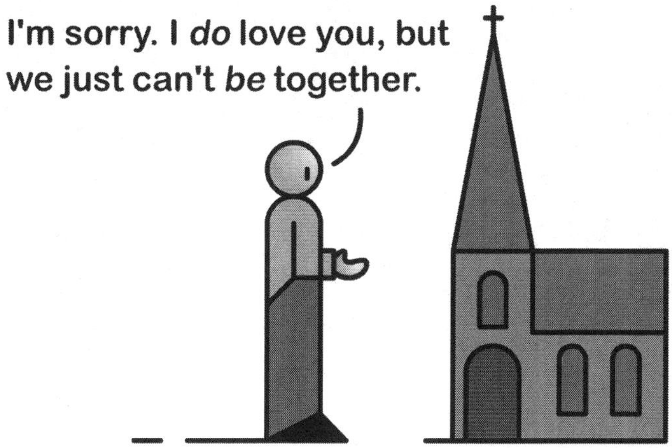
I'm sorry. I *do* love you, but
we just can't *be* together.

Wealth Warning: Real Christianity will seriously damage your wealth.

Contains;
Generosity
Kindness
Hospitality
Sacrifice

Holy Smokes!

I would never wear a cross around my neck.

Why not?

Because people might think I'm a Christian and make all kinds of terrible assumptions about me.

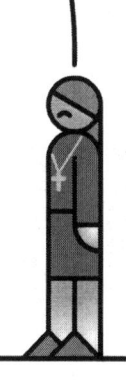

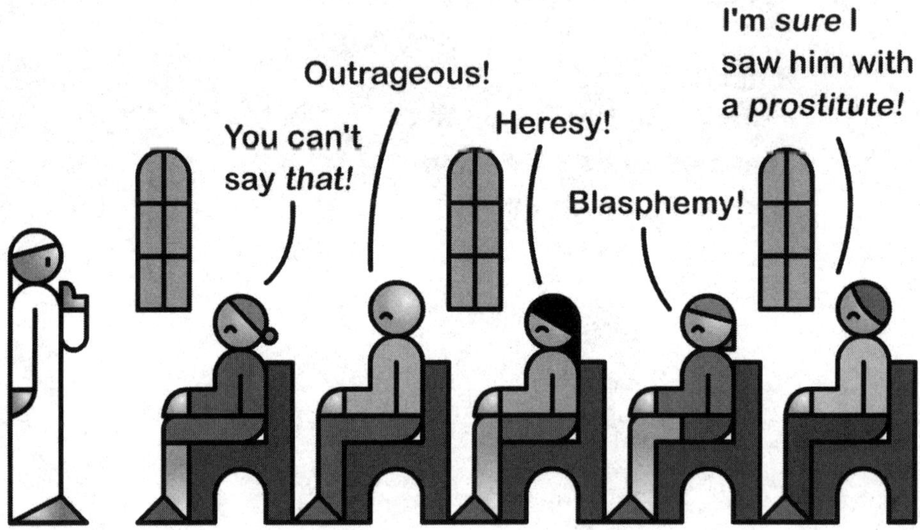

The morning *Jesus* came to preach.

So, which god will you choose?
Will it be generous god number 1...
who says he'll give you anything you want?
Will it be rough, tough god number 2...
who promises to smite your foes and will
always be there to tell you you're right?
Or will it be soft, cuddly god number 3...
who says he'll happily be anything you
want him to be?
The choice is *yours!*

Blind Date!

I am a Post Evangelical, Neo-Calvinist, Emergent Anglican, with a Baptist upbringing and Orthodox sympathies... *Who* did you say *you* were?

Er... Margaret.

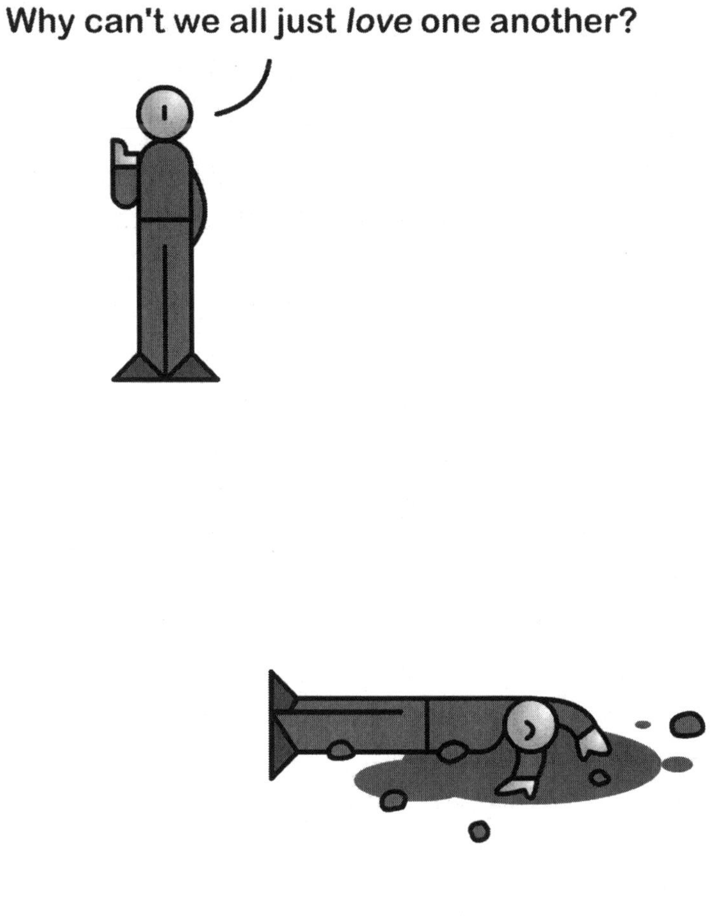
Why can't we all just *love* one another?

Ah, *this* is where *real* life is to be experienced.

Ah, *this* is where *real* life is to be experienced.

Go on, take a bite...
You *know* you *want* to.

Protestants learn very early on that women cannot be trusted.

That Sunday, when the worship band spontaneously combusted...

...was the day I realised there *was* a God.

These worship CD's ensure that all my fields are free from birds for miles around.
I found these useful repellents in my local Christian bookshop.

Worship Leader to Preacher, Worship Leader to Preacher. The people are hyped up and suggestable... Advise we proceed with phase 2, over.
Preacher to Worship Leader. Roger that. I'm going in... They won't know what's *hit them!* Over and out.

How *nice* to meet you... Are you *new* here?
We've been coming here for *years.*

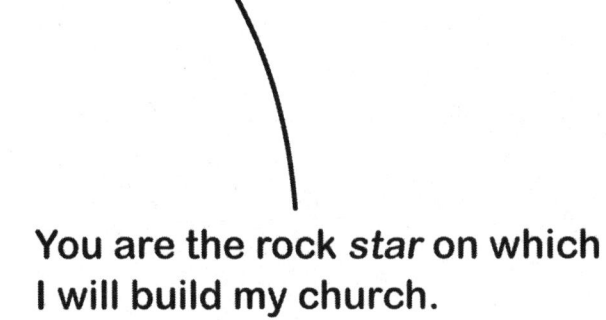

You are the rock *star* on which I will build my church.

Cool.

How worship leaders hear the Lord calling them.

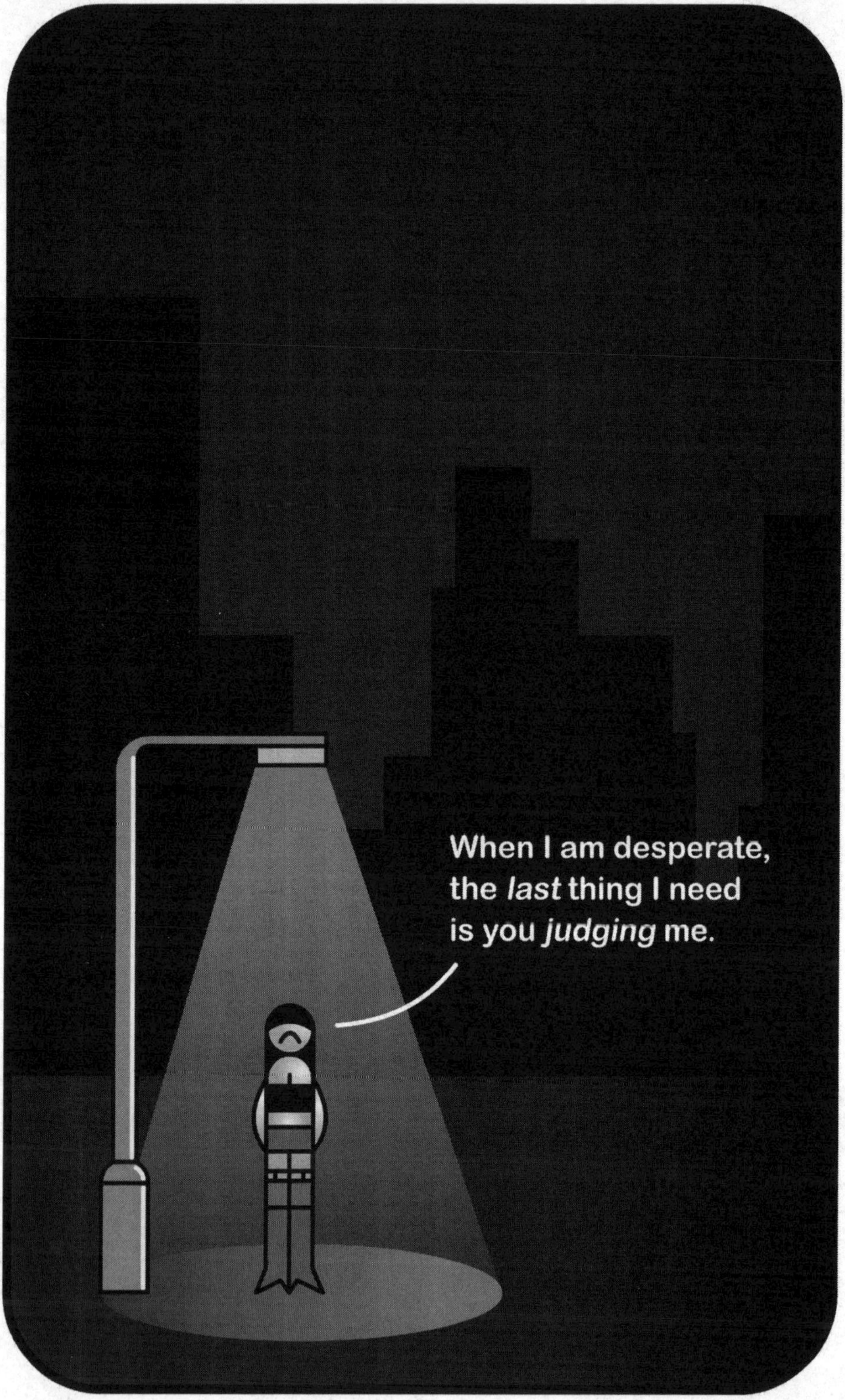
When I am desperate, the *last* thing I need is you *judging* me.

Hey!.. What's *that* you're making?
It's an '*ism*'... When it's *finished* I will *worship* it!

I'm a banker and I'm worth 15 million p.a.
I'm a barmaid and I'm worth minimum wage.
I'm homeless and I'm worth nothing at all.

GET UP!..
IT'S TIME FOR CHURCH!..
YOU'LL BE LATE!
I DON'T WANT TO GO!
YOU HAVE TO GO!..
YOU'RE THE VICAR!

HOW TO DRAW ASBO STYLE

As you can see from these two drawings on the left, making your own ASBO characters is just a piece of cheap software away. With a modicum of effort, you too can draw your own cheeky church characters. Remember, almost everything is drawn using simple circles, squares and triangles, with just a tiny bit of cheating here and there.

Below are a few more examples of typical ASBO Jesus characters and props you may want to try drawing for your own amusement.

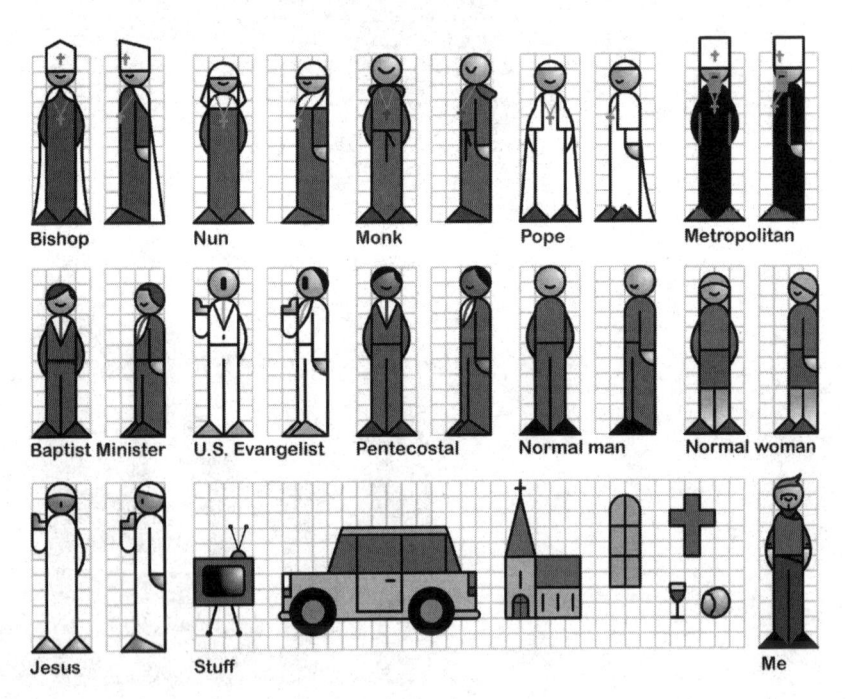

Bishop **Nun** **Monk** **Pope** **Metropolitan**

Baptist Minister **U.S. Evangelist** **Pentecostal** **Normal man** **Normal woman**

Jesus **Stuff** **Me**

I have no idea where I'm going...
Anyone care to join me?